BBL Books

Brad Lewis

Mickey Cohen: The Gangster Squad
and the Mob

The True Story of Vice in Los Angeles

1937-1950

BBL Books

All rights reserved under the International
and Pan-American Copyright Conventions.
Published in the United States by:

BBL Books

www.bradleylewis.org

No part of this publication may be reproduced, stored in a retrieval system, or transmitted, in any form or by any means, electronic, mechanical, photocopying, recording, or otherwise without the written permission
of the author and BBL Books.

Copyright © 2012 by Brad Lewis

First edition
Abridged Version of Hollywood's Celebrity Gangster

Printed in the United States of America

Library of Congress Cataloging-in-Publication Data

Lewis, Bradley.

1. Cohen, Mickey, 1914–1976. 2. Criminals--California--Los Angeles--Biography. 3. Gangsters--California--Los Angeles--Biography. 4. Jewish criminals--United States--Biography. 5. Organized crime--California--Los Angeles--History.
HV6248.C64 L49 2007 364.109/2

For MR

The criminal has no hates or fears—except very personal ones. He is possibly the only human left in the world who looks lovingly on society.

—Ben Hecht
Screenwriter and author

1.

Twenty-five-year-old Mickey traveled west with a man identified as Joe Gentile, a career player for Capone. The young entrepreneur and his older domo pal established a base of operations at a modest Los Angeles hotel. Under the watchful eye of Joe G., as some knew him, Mickey initially supported himself with heavy work, the usual stickup activity. He was happy to be back with his remaining family in Los Angeles, and enjoyed the southern California climate while adjusting to the rapidly changing city.

When he arrived, Los Angeles was still raw, and made for criminals. Helen Gahagan Douglas, a former actress and representative from Los Angeles' Fourteenth District, knew the fragile landscape: "Frances Starr hadn't exaggerated when she said that Hollywood Boulevard resembled a movie set built to collapse the moment the stage manager cried, 'Strike it!'" The expansive locale was easy prey for Mickey and his East Coast contacts.[1]

Los Angeles was a town without rules, where bookmakers operated in the open and slot machines were rampant. A recall ousted corrupt Mayor Frank Shaw; he was replaced with Judge Fletcher Bowron. Shaw, who had been in the supermarket business with his brother Joe, operated with the local Sicilians, who ran an unsophisticated yet controlling interest in the West.

Some, like singer Lorna's father, producer Sid Luft, who favored a more provincial description of Los Angeles, were in denial about the criminal activities: "This was a very, very clean town. Nothing like Detroit or Chicago."[2]

In 1937, Los Angeles police squad cars responded to 83,315 calls that resulted in 17,529 arrests, too much for local jails. Sheriff Eugene "Gene" Biscailuz was pleased with his overcrowded operation at the Hall of Justice, and emphasized that any cook who worked for him had to be "proud of his [membership] card." During this period, Biscailuz began a relationship as Mickey's "father confessor." Mickey frequently flashed his own miniature Highway Patrol badge, supplied by the sheriff.[3]

Illegal gambling clubs, the principle form of entertainment, lined the Sunset Strip and nearby towns like Redondo Beach and Culver City, the latter home to MGM studios.[4] Tango parlors filled the adjoining beautiful Manhattan Beach, a community that boasted of its madam, who attended all the city council meetings. The police and local governments allowed the Hollywood mob full run of the little cities at night. The Los Angeles police had no rights on the politically independent Strip. Only Sheriff Biscailuz had jurisdiction over the bookmakers, madams, and after-hour joints. The symbiotic relationship between the sheriff and the mob had existed for years.

The misogynist Hollywood era was also in its heyday. Los Angeles was a Sodom and Gomorrah, filled with tens of thousands of girls who flocked to town to become the next Betty Grable, the sexy pinup with the sensational legs. Author Lee Mortimer described the city as an "Elysian fields for lonely-heart and introduction clubs, many palpable call services."

From the day he arrived, Mickey was all over town in fancy clothes and cars. He was out every night, playing the role of the consummate schmoozer; he knew how to work the glitzy crowd as well as anyone. He recalled: "I was out with ten different broads every night, and I was in every cabaret..."

However, he had practical business realities to overcome; he was technically working for Bugsy, with whom he didn't rush to solidify his relationship. "Actually we never even gave a fuck about Benny. We were just rooting, just taking off scores..." During his early tenure, Mickey learned that his former girlfriend Georgia, from Cleveland, had taken ill. He performed extra heists to send her money.

Handsome and somewhat smooth-talking Bugsy had started his operations at his sister's house at chic 721 N. Doheny Drive in Beverly Hills. He immediately held a meeting with all the top mobsters and brazenly let them know that he planned to organize their operations, and that he was the sole and final arbiter of anything illegal.

George "Les" Bruneman, part of the old-time Crawford-McAfee mob that operated gaming clubs in the resort areas south of Los Angeles, didn't agree with the new splits offered by Bugsy. Bruneman had aspirations of controlling all the gambling operations in southern California. On July 19, 1937, a little over a month after Bugsy had hit town, three bullets hit Bruneman while he walked on the promenade at Redondo Beach, forty-five minutes south of Hollywood. He stumbled into a local movie house and an ambulance was summoned. He remarkably survived a punctured lung, and defiantly announced he was going to reopen his clubs, after spending six weeks in the hospital. On October 25, eleven shots caught him while he drank at the Roost Café on West Temple Street. The five assailants also wounded his blonde nurse Alice

Ingram and killed an innocent bystander, who had tried to record the license plate number on the getaway car. After Bruneman fell to the floor, two of the assailants drew forty-five automatics; one shooter handled two guns, and the duo pumped another five shots into Bruneman to guarantee the job. Bruneman, armed with two guns, had just bought a round of drinks for the fifteen patrons. Italian mob leader Jack Dragna and Bugsy purportedly paid off notorious hit man and future FBI informant Frank "The Bomp" Bompensiero three days later. Bugsy and Tony "The Hat" Cornero (Stralla) now had full reign in the little beach communities, something Mickey would capitalize on.[5]

The more macabre aspects of taking control slowly surfaced; the newspapers began to cover more murders and beatings. It wasn't all Mickey's doing or influence; some revisionists even link him to the Bruneman murder, but he spent much time answering questions at police stations. Within a year of his arrival, he and his ruffians pulled over eighty stickups without a single arrest. His later arrest record included three for bookmaking, two for cutting phone wires, assault with a deadly weapon, and vagrancy. Police released him the same day as most of his arrests. He had already learned the power of legal, police, and political connections.

Independent-thinking Mickey, of course, had checked in with Bugsy, as per the agreement with Lansky. He kept his distance, reserving judgment and comments on Bugsy's style and personality, while both dressed-to-the-nines newcomers ingratiated themselves with the movie stars. Siegel said of him, "I like his balls, and I think Mickey can be a big help to me." Once he and Bugsy had a working relationship, Bugsy would ask him to handle certain jobs, like sticking a joint on the Sunset Strip owned by Eddie Neales, who was a friend of writer Milton Holmes, and played tennis at the Beverly Hills Tennis Club, to the dismay of many of the members. The club had accused Neales of skimming off the top of charity events held at the posh watering hole.

The stickup on the Strip was a classic Hollywood job. Mickey held a gun on the ritzy patrons while everyone handed over their money and jewelry. The miniature hardnose glanced over at a good-looking broad, but resisted temptation, since it was not polite to socialize while holding a shotgun. Outside one of his bruisers told him that they had just held up musician and bandleader Harry James and actress Betty Grable.

Years later when Mickey became one of the darlings of the social scene, he found himself at a gathering with Grable and his friend Florabel Muir, who thought the reunion with Grable was funny, and reminded him that he had once robbed her. Mickey, always conscious of his image, tried to apologize for his past, and said that perhaps he wasn't even at the scene of the crime.

Grable whispered in his ear, "We were insured anyway."

Bugsy and Mickey were not in Los Angeles to promote the heist business. Their larger job was to infiltrate the Italian mob and see how much they could carve out for the Jews. Mickey specialized in gambling, by now somewhat of an expert. The Sicilians were not pleased with Bugsy and Mickey's activities, and certainly did not want to share the movie business or gambling coffers. Mickey and Bugsy's formidable adversary was Jack Dragna, and he would play a significant role in Mickey's rise to power. Despite descriptions as an Italian relic, a Mustache Pete who was unwilling to flow with the new corporate tide, short-tempered Dragna was a big earner for the family and no pushover. The traditional ways of the Italian mob would prove an arduous challenge, but it appeared that he and the other Italians had underestimated the Jews.

Mickey, who had ties to both the Italian and Jewish mobs, was not afraid of Dragna. From his jail cell, Charles "Lucky" Luciano (Salvatore Lucania) sent word to Dragna to back off and let

Bugsy and Mickey set up their operations. Luciano originally had said that Bugsy "was heading west for his health and the health of all of us."[6]

Before Mickey's arrival, Dragna looked to mobster Johnny Rosselli (Filippo Sacco) for regular advice and physical help in modernizing the bookmaking and gambling operations. Handsome, smooth-talking Rosselli had already established himself as a big player with the movie studios. He extorted millions from their coffers by providing protection to movie moguls. Rosselli was no fan of the new Jews, but he mostly stayed out of Mickey's way, and often cooperated.[7]

The criminal power transition followed a logical course. The new Jewish mobsters pretended to ingratiate themselves with the Italians, while their main goal was to diminish, partner when necessary, or eliminate them. To accomplish their goals, they needed strong liaisons with the growing legitimate businesses.

If Mickey and Bugsy were to move up, they needed to court the local luminaries on a regular basis.[8] The real power brokers in town were movie moguls like Louis B. Mayer, Jack Warner, and Harry Cohn, each with his own police force.[9] Bugsy's first substantial business contacts were Warner and Mayer, two of the most powerful Jewish studio bosses. Actor George Raft made certain that Harry

Cohn was also accessible to Bugsy. (Raft lived in an old world luxuriously decorated apartment across the street from Romanoff's, a popular restaurant.)[10] The studio bosses appeared glad to have Bugsy in town, particularly after the years of Sicilian extortion. The moguls now had a direct pipeline at the local level to the growing national Jewish syndicate. In exchange for that luxury, Bugsy and Mickey controlled the extras who appeared in the movies, a nickel-and-dime extortion racket that added up. Mickey set up the more lucrative "insurance business," having the moguls fork over big bucks to guarantee smooth sailing on the elaborate sound stages.

Sam Giancana's nephew (godson) and half-brother, Sam and Chuck, acknowledged the movie business cornerstone and the symbiotic relationship with the mob: "Mooney [Giancana] told Chuck that the studios were too lucrative to abandon. 'We're not about to turn our back on so much money and power...they're our friends now. Rosselli's got them in his pocket.'" The list included Harry Cohn, Harry Warner, and L. B. Mayer—Columbia, Warner Brothers, and MGM. The mob boys had their fingers in a large pie.

Mickey would soon meet all the studio bosses, and he would do favors for them, particularly Cohn, who was a notorious bully, famous for his vulgar remarks and behavior: "If you've got talent, I'll lick your ass, but if you don't I'll kick it." He was one of the first Hollywood characters to use "fuck" in routine conversation.

Mickey initially was more comfortable with many of the studio bosses and their ilk rather than organization leaders or other legitimate industry owners, and capitalized immediately on the familiar speech patterns and prevailing business attitudes.

He quickly latched onto the parallels between organized crime and show business. The show business wannabees were bright, but didn't do well in school, and often shied away from books in order to favor their own creative fantasies. Entertainment and organized crime nurtured each other's business interests, and attracted a coterie of shady characters who legitimized their activities in the movie business with panjandrums like "manager" and "producer."[11] The mob easily exploited the creative pool. Many of them were fond of mobsters, along with everything else connected to the entertainment business, from theater tickets to transportation.[12]

Mickey and Bugsy acted swiftly to move in on all the ripe existing businesses. Like Bugsy, Mickey was a front man assigned to report on the prevailing attitudes and possibilities for the growing Jewish mob, which offered management advice. The concomitant political infiltration process required a lot of glad-handing and graft. The locals were already used to having thugs around, mostly of a less polished variety than Bugsy and even Mickey. For many, the new Jewish boys were a breath of fresh air. Having a ready supply of out of town muscle to back up threats of violence helped get the fledgling Jewish mob off the ground.

During Mickey's first year in Los Angeles, he met brown-eyed LaVonne, an Irish Catholic. Author Reid highlighted the love-at-first-sight romance:

> If Mickey Cohen ever loved anybody more than himself it must have been LaVonne Norma Weaver, a pretty little redhead and fashion model just out of high school when she met the hoodlum in the Bandbox Club in Los Angeles.[13]

The love-smitten Hollywoodite said this, and little more, about his first meeting with LaVonne: "She was some kind of dance instructor at some of the studios. She had me intrigued, because she also flew a plane and all that bullshit." (Since she was still alive when Mickey's scant autobiography finally appeared, he wisely felt protective of her, and supplied minimal personal detail about their relationship.)

LaVonne, who also modeled teen-age dresses, was going steady with a pilot, but Mickey soon changed all that. He knew he had to make a good impression. On his first date with her, he insists that there was no dancing, handholding, or passes. But he did arrive for the date at 11 p.m., four hours late. The couple stopped at his residence, smoke-filled by his waiting pals. After an hour of introductions, he treated her to dinner "at the best place in town."

Mickey craved respectability and social acceptance, and knew that a gun moll would dash his hopes. LaVonne fit his idea of a proper girlfriend; she quickly became part of his life. She could pass for a debutante or finishing school graduate, compared to most of the club girls. Her voice indicated a cultured background, and at least she spoke proper English. She was not shy about correcting his speech, or asking him to improve his diction.

One Passover after Mickey's arrival, he sent for longtime pal Hooky Rothman. "You gonna have it good here," Mickey told Hooky while he was still at the Santa Fe railroad station.

Not everyone shared Mickey's assessment of Los Angeles. He encountered many East Coast show business people who were initially disappointed in Hollywood dreamland, a place they had flocked to in order to beat the oppressive system found in more established East Coast cities. Los Angeles Jews were a subculture of dreamers, who had unrealistic expectations about the glamorous new digs. Hollywood life proved simultaneously to be the solution and the new problem; it required substantive socioeconomic adjustments. Mickey had one leg up on the bewildered East Coast crowd; he was already familiar with the expansive terrain, which was devoid of a cultural backbone. Intellectual expectations didn't encumber him; he was there to make the money.

Mickey's Jewish identity remained the foundation of his personal sensibilities. Larger Los Angeles was not a Jewish-friendly city. The prevailing attitudes toward Jews were negative, fueled by old political and social theories. Anti-Semitism ran deep within the Mafia, who often blamed the Jews for committing the crimes. Some theorists claim that the Mafia ultimately exploited the Jews for their age-old stereotypical financial skills. Regardless, legitimate Jewish and non-Jewish businesses increasingly embraced Jewish criminals for protection; mom-and-pop stores and restaurants had to show allegiance to either the Jews or Italians in order to survive.

Anti-Semitism was so pervasive that Jewish women lied about their religion in order to get employment; many corporations did not hire Jews. Areas like Beverly Hills and Brentwood, despite their growing Jewish populations, were decidedly Christian. All schools sung religious hymns at Christmas, and the Reformed Wilshire Boulevard Temple was a controversial example of assimilation, with its churchlike environment and choir.

Zionist-leaning Mickey shared Bugsy's interest in Jewish causes, particularly in view of the recent success of Adolf Hitler. Many Jewish syndicate executives paid close attention to overseas activities affecting Jews. Bugsy had his own brand of Jewish political activism. In 1937, he stayed at the same villa in Italy as two Nazi leaders, and promptly informed his hostess, Dorothy DiFrasso, that he was planning to knock off both Germans. DiFrasso, Count DiFrasso's wife, had invited him to visit at the same time that the Count was entertaining Joseph Goebbels and Hermann Göring, respectively Hitler's propaganda minister and air force leader.[14]

"You can't do that!" replied the Countess.

Bugsy didn't understand and answered, "Sure I can. It's an easy set-up the way they're walking around here." Movie mogul Jack Warner was in town promoting *The Life of Emile Zola* and was privy to Bugsy's assassination plans. Bugsy called Lansky for permission to bump off Mussolini too. Lansky told him that he was operating independently, and not to contact any local Mafia. Warner singlehandedly prevented Bugsy from breaking up the Rome-Berlin Axis. His take was all Hollywood: "I talked him out of it on the grounds we couldn't fix the local harness bulls if we got caught."

On November 9, 1938, Hitler put his political theories into practical use. Kristallnacht, the Night of the Broken Glass, witnessed the unleashing of Nazi mobs in Germany and in Austria, eager to torch synagogues, break shop windows, and beat anyone suspected of being Jewish. Over one hundred Jews died that night, marking the beginning of the Holocaust. Things would change forever, abroad and in the United States, inside and outside the mob.[15]

Mickey was not an observant Jew and had abandoned daily Jewish traditions. Nevertheless, the catastrophic event had a profound affect on his beliefs and he, like many Jewish mobsters, would keep a close watch on world Jewish affairs and future Zionist activities.

The raw Angeleno had to find a way to succeed during the worst of times for Jews, and his Jewish defense interests took hold early. He wrote of an episode with a man named Robert Noble, described as having "a lot of notoriety." Public figure Noble was notorious for his outspoken views as a Nazi Bundist, member of the subversive association Friends of

Progress, and had the attention of radio and newspapers to spew his venom; Mickey called it "rabble-rousing anti-Jew" sentiments. During a temporary incarceration, which included lengthy questioning, he encountered Noble and another man. Recognizing them, he arranged to have the men put in a cell with him, and then he mercilessly beat both of them under the auspices of the police. The two men, face to face with snarling Mickey, tried to move toward the perimeter of the cell, which the police had locked.

Mickey's enthusiasm for these altercations comes through in his memoir. He was proud of his early reputation as a *bulvan*—Yiddish for "crude ox." "I started bouncing their heads together," recalled Mickey. "With the two of them, you'd think they'd put up a fight, but they didn't do nothing." Mickey's embellishments continued:

> So I'm going over them pretty good. The windup is that they're climbing up on the bars...they're screaming and hollering so much everybody thinks it's a riot... The jail chief... Bright comes running down himself...he can't get in. These two guys are still up on the bars screaming about their rights and, "Why did ya throw us in with an animal, with a crazy man?"... I've gone back to my corner and picked up the

newspaper... He comes over and says, "You son of a bitch, what happened now?"

Mickey remained calm, knowing that he had the cooperation of the police. "What are you asking me for? I'm sitting here reading the newspaper. Them two guys got into a fight with each other..."

Nothing came of it since he convinced the police that the men were anti-American and anti-General McArthur. In 1942, authorities put Noble in prison for sedition.

The undersized *shtarker*—"tough guy"—earned a reputation as an enforcer for politically correct causes. Mickey's strong political feelings were public knowledge, and he would continue his involvement as a lobbyist. Anti-Nazi activity was growing throughout the country, and he received requests from organizations like the Writers Guild for help in dealing with Nazi infiltrators. He and his goons assisted frightened local authorities in breaking up Nazi meetings. Since he had no interest in the civil rights of anti-Semites, he proved the right party for the job.

Hollywood and Los Angeles was his world to succeed or fail. With Bugsy taking the lead, it appeared Mickey had really struck gold.

2.

Word of Mickey's early business success naturally traveled east, and he became a host for the boys from out of town, many eager to meet the bosses in the movie industry. He didn't entertain in his home since his guests, "...wanted to see a broad." He had no problem in that arena: he had a stable of "...starlets—little broads—around. I don't mean whores, at times they were what you call, call girls..." Despite his and many of his friends' denials, he quickly established himself as a pimp. He also organized a unique welcome service for tourist mobsters: he would supply them with transportation and weapons.

Mickey emulated the conventional corporate style. He first treated a guest to dinner, and then they exchanged money. There were train junkets to New York, elaborate parties on their way to a prizefight or to nowhere. The boys played cards, often with some of the top business people and gamblers from Los Angeles.

Folklore credits gambler Nick "Nick the Greek" Dandolas for Mickey's lightning-fast entry into racetrack bookmaking. The well-read Greek was full of philosophical stories about long life, and told Mickey how a sect in India regularly lived to be 180 by eating certain breads and breathing correctly. Mickey stuck with ice cream.

"You're doing it all the hard way," said the Greek. "A smart kid doesn't have to go on the heavy to make a living."

The Brown Derby restaurant meeting with the Greek changed Mickey's life and business focus. He accepted the parental advice, and developed more businesses that did not require a financial exchange at gunpoint. Within three days, he set up shop as a bookmaker, only a few yards from the racetrack, in full view of Pinkerton detectives.

The nouveau bookie expanded his gambling interests to meet local needs and national plans. In 1938, he began an extensive betting operation in Westwood, the village west of Beverly Hills, and home to UCLA.

In order to monitor the boxing action, particularly ancillary gambling and fixes, Mickey hung out at Olympic Stadium in Los Angeles, located south of Pico Boulevard at Sixteenth and Grand streets, in an area known for its cheap bars and hotels. Whenever he frequented the bouts, an entourage of pretty women, bodyguards, and bail bondsmen surrounded him. Associate and bondsman Abe Phillips watched the count on the till and fixes, while Harry Pregerson, then a law student, would help keep Mickey out of jail.

The Phillips socialized frequently with Mickey. Abe's wife Helen knew that he enjoyed teasing and she joked at his expense, "Go out and kill me a couple of people." Mickey had already developed an unusual sense of humor for someone in his line of work, and appeared tickled by Helen.

While Mickey's short arms stretched into every aspect of gambling, authorities had to take a public stance to satisfy complaining constituents. Sheriff Biscailuz created a special vice squad to deal with the gambling boom, and made it mandatory for any raid to target gambling joints. The offshore gambling boat *Rex*, docked neatly beyond the three-point-one-mile offshore limit, coyly operated under Biscailuz's nose for a few seasons. The *Rex*, represented by attorney Sam Rummel, had its own horse room that paid track odds, luring customers away from the local racetracks. Former San Francisco cab driver Tony Cornero ran the *Rex* and would later build the Stardust Hotel in Vegas. Bugsy had fifteen percent of the *Rex* action.

State Attorney General Earl Warren declared the *Rex* inside California territory and not in federal waters. Police launched a well-publicized raid on the boat from coastline headquarters at the Santa Monica Del Mar Hotel. The sheriff and his staff enjoyed regular long stays at the beach to protect the interests of local citizens. The resultant Keystone Cop raid, with fire hoses streaming water down on the little police launch, ended with the beleaguered press receiving free imported brandy, thrown overboard to their hired boats. A few gambling devices were seized, and the reporters called it a night. According to Florabel Muir, who attended the raids, a more accessible offshore boat, the *Texas*, "got the works." By 1939, all the gambling boats were gone, and the mob concentrated on its land-based gambling enterprises.

Since Mickey had acquired an independent streak that was somewhat tolerated back east, he didn't waste any time establishing this same reputation in Los Angeles. He robbed one of boss Dragna's bookmaking operations belonging to Louis Merli (also known as Salvatore "Dago Louie" Piscopo), a partner of Johnny Rosselli. Author James Morton described Mickey in those early years as "essentially wild, a killer, and a freelancer."[16]

The heist took place while two sheriff's deputies watched the joint, a thirty-phone shop. A sawed-off shotgun and the requisite revolvers got everyone's attention. The take was about thirty grand and some jewelry. After the robbery, word got back to Mickey that he should check in with Bugsy, who had arranged a meeting with Rosselli at attorney Jerry Geisler's office in Los Angeles. Geisler always took care of Mickey and Bugsy, but according to Mickey, "I wouldn't really call Jerry Geisler a mob attorney."[17]

At the Geisler meeting, Bugsy made it clear that Mickey screwed up by robbing one of Rosselli's boys. Bugsy, in accordance with Rosselli, wanted Mickey to kick back some or all of the score. It didn't sit well with Mickey; mobsters didn't kick back score money to anyone. As a token gesture of respect, he returned a tiepin that had sentimental value, and avoided a battle with Rosselli and Dragna. Rosselli, unlike Dragna, let cooler heads prevail, preferring to build an alliance with his new colleagues, rarely appearing self-motivated. Although the anger simmered, Bugsy and Mickey worked harder to control all the action by muscling in on Dragna's territory.

New jugular blood spilled through the Hollywood area, while Mickey expertly played both sides of the mob. He diminished his stickup work, focused more on gambling, and came to the rescue of other businesses, particularly if run by Jews. He offered protection against other bad guys who were also trying to make a living like him.

One of Mickey's competitors, Irish Jimmy Fox, was harassing two small Jewish independent bookmakers, who ran a legitimate drugstore near Beverly Hills, at San Vicente and Wilshire boulevards. Fox, like his predecessors, made money by muscling small business owners to pay protection money.

Mickey particularly disliked Fox. "He was a two-gun son of a bitch, and he carried a lot of weight around here—kind of like a czar."

The two bookies didn't like Fox or his deal, and they complained to an intermediary who appealed to Fox. Mickey was all ears when the same source contacted him, and he met with the bookies at bandleader Mike Lyman's restaurant.

Because of his mixed morality and bias, Mickey defended the bookies, and told them, "Ya tell him ya spoke to me, and ya tell him I said to take a good fuck for himself, and tell him it come from me."

He arranged a follow-up meeting with Fox at the home of one of the Jewish bookies. Fox bellowed something about Mickey's brother Harry, who had stiffed him on a bootleg deal.

Following words to this effect, "My feelings towards you ain't so goddamn good anyway," miniature tough guy Mickey shot Fox.

According to Mickey, Fox's wounds were minimal. That night, the police arrested Mickey during a prizefight at the Olympic Auditorium, and led him to believe that he had killed Fox. The resolution was typical for Mickey: no charges filed. Fox lived on and never bothered Mickey or the two Jewish bookmakers again.

Local problems like Fox and Bruneman did not require national intervention, but occasionally the front office contacted Bugsy and Mickey to deal with someone of waning popularity. During the initial productive years of the Mickey and Bugsy Show,[18] Harry "Big Greenie" Greenberg's (George Schachter) mob value diminished on both coasts, and he was "going." He had crossed mob leader Lepke, and had threatened to talk with New York District Attorney Thomas E. Dewey. Mickey originally had orders to monitor Greenberg, but his career was no longer salvageable.

Popular movie culture displayed Greenberg as a cuddly teddy bear of a victim who naively felt protected by Bugsy. Big Greenie was not naive, but had mistakenly played the authorities against the mob.

The word was passed down: "Keep him in tow until we get a couple of boys out there."

First Lepke put a hit out on Big Greenie, but it failed. Greenie left New York following deportation to his native Poland, lived under his real name, Schachter, in Montreal, and ultimately fled to Hollywood. Everyone above Bugsy in the syndicate no longer saw Greenie as a threat, and decided to leave him alone, and "give him a pass." Bugsy still wanted Greenie out of the way and made up his mind to get rid of him. Mickey likely knew Greenie's schedule; he left the safe house every night to drive to the drugstore to get a newspaper. Forty-eight-year-old Greenie was a sitting duck the Wednesday night of November 22, 1939. Big Greenie was peacefully reading the morning newspaper when he was gunned down in his car. Mrs. Ida Schachter dressed in black for the inquest when she stated that she was unaware of her deceased husband's past.

Bugsy's murder indictment materialized in August 1940, along with Frankie Carbo, Mendy Weiss (acting boss of Murder, Inc.), and Harry "Champ" Segal.[19] Brownsville-born Abe "Kid Twist" Reles had already given his deposition, and hoped for clemency. He had admitted being in on the hit, and planned to testify that Bugsy had grown impatient and fired on Big Greenie. Brooklyn District Attorney William O'Dwyer had publicized Reles' cooperation, thereby infuriating Bugsy. Worse, O'Dwyer's assistant Burton Turkus, hardly a politician like his boss, wanted to pursue the case.

Somebody threw Reles from a hotel window in Brooklyn, resulting in a rash of jokes about the singing canary who couldn't fly. Police Captain Frank Bals was responsible for Reles' safety, and concluded that his death was an accident. Turkus knew that Reles would not have risked his life on a bed sheet and some wire—the reported material for his failed and deadly escape. Bals, rumored to be a bagman for the mob, was appointed deputy police commissioner by then Mayor O'Dwyer in 1945.

Bugsy remained in jail while he awaited the trial. He wore a custom-made denim jail uniform, had a private valet (another prisoner) who shined his shoes, and unlimited free phone calls. Ciro's owner Billy Wilkerson, jumpy, compulsive gambler, and Bugsy pal, saw to it that the Ciro's chef sent Bugsy his lavish meals of steak and pheasant.[20] During the forty-nine-day jail stint, Bugsy made eighteen visits to Dr. Allen Black, his Beverly Hills dentist. During one of his nights out, he dined at trendy Lindy's restaurant with English film actress Wendy Barrie. When Sheriff Biscailuz got wind of the rendezvous, he blamed the jail doctor Benjamin Blank, rather than face the corruption in his own sheriff's office. Dr. Blank wasn't so squeaky clean, on the take for over thirty grand from Bugsy, and lost his job, only to end up at MGM studios. He was well connected: he had gone to medical school with Bugsy's brother,

Dr. Maurice Siegel! Dr. Siegel practiced in L. A. County.

Mickey claimed that Murder Inc.'s Allie Tannenbaum had murdered Big Greenie. Tannenbaum naturally testified that he was innocent, and pinned the whole thing on Carbo and Bugsy, whom he placed behind the wheel of the old Ford getaway car. The stolen hit guns originated at a cargo pier in New York, courtesy of Longie Zwillman, someone beholden to Bugsy.[21]

Bugsy wisely hired Jerry Geisler to defend him; everyone got off. Geisler received $30,000 from Bugsy, who had withdrawn the money from the campaign contribution to District Attorney Dockweiler's fund.

Not all Bugsy's problems with the law were as complicated or as serious as the Greenie trial. George Raft, who rivaled Sinatra for ties to the mob, appeared as a witness for Bugsy at a Beverly Hills trial, and put on quite a show. The judge reduced the felony charges to a bookmaking misdemeanor, a paltry $250 fine.[22]

By this time, inextricable bonds linked Mickey and Bugsy's daily lives. The most unflattering version of their relationship describes Bugsy as Mickey's role model. Authors have called Mickey a shadow, bodyguard, chauffeur, gopher, and lieutenant. Underachiever Mickey saw himself as a lead player, albeit a character actor with a dangerous independent streak.

Nevertheless, Mickey and Bugsy worked together to insure their infiltration of the Sicilian operation. The takeover process was rocky, although the affable duo gave off appearances of an easy life; they were out on the town every night. Bugsy and Mickey were not shy about taking over, nor was either reticent when it came to establishing a classy public image. Many Italians didn't understand Mickey because he wooed the newspapers. That disturbed Dragna, who felt Mickey threatened everyone's success.

Dragna wasn't afraid and didn't back off as instructed by Luciano. On occasion he incorrectly described his position as secure:

> Meyer's [Lansky] got a Jewish family built along the same lines as our thing. But his family's all over the country. He's got guys like Lou Rhody and Dalitz, Doc Stacher, Gus Greenbaum, sharp fucking guys, good businessmen, and they know better than try to fuck us.[23]

Dragna became the butt of jokes, and proved no match for Mickey's tenaciousness.

To further irritate Dragna, and deflect public ire away from the Jewish mob, Mickey made statements to the effect that the Italians were ruining the neighborhood, and he was performing a public service through his adversarial activities. He told newspaper editor and old friend Jim Richardson, "The people of Los Angeles ought to get down on their knees and thank God for Mickey Cohen because if it wasn't for me the Wops would have this town tied up." He bucked the old world Sicilian system while currying favor with the public by pretending to ward off the elder Italian mob. Bugsy's attitude toward the local establishment, particularly Dragna, was "fuck 'em," and stood behind Mickey's every move.[24]

Mickey made certain that the newspapers printed positive quotes about his quick rise in the local business world:

> Since I have been in charge of the program there has been a definite reduction in the crime of this city. All the types of people who would under previous conditions be bustin' heads in dark alleys and breakin' into respectable homes for robbery are now on my payroll... [He meant many of the Italians, too] ...and don't have to do that sort of thing to make a living. I've been a boon to this town. And I'll tell you somethin.' Despite the attitude of the police, there are a lot a people beginning to realize that fact.

He wasn't far off from the truth, since many local citizens accepted him, and he was already a Hollywood fixture.

However, certain national goals required a synergetic effort. A project brewed through the early forties that would revolutionize several industries and repaint the canvas of our country with an indelible vice-tainted patina. The growing Jewish syndicate needed Dragna's help with that new venture. Dragna was no beauty queen, and Bugsy was a good-looking, more articulate poster boy for gambling, someone the Hollywood crowd would follow to the proposed fantasyland. Dragna was incapable of providing public relations for the development of Las Vegas, so Bugsy used him principally for his California contacts and muscle.

The psychological and practical needs of Bugsy and Dragna initially complemented each other, and set the wheels in motion for developing Las Vegas. Both men envisioned themselves as leaders, a convenient stance for an awkward partnership. Neither party had much of a choice; both national mobs had an interest in expanding Nevada gambling. A unified commission on organized gambling had taken place in Atlantic City. Dragna attended the meeting and accepted his role, despite his distrust for the Jews, whom he thought were unorganized and uncontrollable.

The Atlantic City conclave had determined how to structure the Annenberg Nationwide News service (race wire) to benefit gambling. Bookies needed properly timed information on sporting events, particularly horse racing. One of the reasons Bugsy was sent to California was to help set up the race wire business, which was sorely lacking by East Coast standards. Securing the race wire became part of Mickey's job description. He made inroads to control the growing wire activity around Los Angeles. Many legitimate people owned a piece of the countrywide gold mine. The national and local fighting became extensive; local infighting resulted in beatings and murder, and until now did not attract much national media attention. Mickey grew uncomfortable with the wire service wars, but remained dedicated to developing gambling clubs on the California coast, and cooperated with national needs to secure the wire trade.[25]

At the same time, Los Angeles escalated its social and business transformation. Organized crime naturally moved in on the new theaters, restaurants, clubs, and movie business, creating a symbiosis that would continue for decades. Aside from influencing the talent bookers, the mob controlled the dinnerware, glassware, and napkins.

Entertainment and organized crime learned to get along.

Nightclubs had become an integral part of popular culture in Los Angeles. Tuxedos were the standard attire for all employees. Sexy cigarette girls sashayed between the tables, while camera girls solicited business, too. A discreet "sawbuck" (ten dollars) slipped to the maître d' and he would open the velvet rope leading to the best tables. Money laundering and illegal gambling took place under the nose of politicians and police. Mickey saw nightclubs and restaurants as more than a place to socialize. He wanted, and ultimately received, a piece of the action.[26]

The Sunset Strip area was the hot ticket that provided a small-town feel. Never again would the country see the strange nighttime intermingling of movie stars, mobsters, politicians, restaurateurs, and the filthy rich. The extensive club scene helped fuel the development of the entertainment business.

Writer Lloyd Shearer detailed the odd mix of elements in a night out on the town:

> ...the studios were run by pirates, semi-illiterates, amoral immigrants, men who indulged in corruption, blackmail, sex orgies, nepotism, men who made exorbitant profits...and trafficked

with the most despicable segments of the underworld.

Despite Mickey's East Coast tutoring and his hard-earned street education, he still had a lot to learn about Hollywood and its luminaries. An early lesson materialized about actors' unwillingness to pick up checks. His run-in was with Jackie Gleason (Herbert John Gleason), also from a crummy section of Brooklyn. During a party night at one of Mickey's new restaurants, big mouth funny lady Martha Raye, playboy attorney Gregson "Greg" Bautzer, and Gleason ordered everything on the menu. Mickey was happy because he had discovered how hard it was to make legitimate money in the restaurant business. When the sloshed group rose to leave, Gleason, "The Great One," merely signed his name to the check.

Mickey was livid. "I never heard of signing the check in my life."

It got worse as the group made its way to the front door.

"What is this bullshit? You come in here and eat and drink and you sign—who the hell signs a check?" screamed Mickey.

Gleason bellowed back, "Don't you know who I am?"

An argument ensued, and Mickey threatened Gleason. Martha Raye called Mickey every name in the book. When Bautzer stepped in to guarantee the meal with his check, Mickey held his ground and yelled, "Who the fuck are you?"[27]

The homunculus restaurateur liked to say that he slapped around former boxer Gleason, who once took on the Joe Louis adversary Tony Galento in the streets.

The Strip became Mickey's roving office. Anytime he showed up out on the town, owners feared a problem, but most were happy to have a customer who spread around cash as if he was printing it at home, a business he always personally avoided. During these late night jaunts, he claimed that he rarely had a drink, despite conflicting reports about his alcohol consumption. Certainly, heavy drinking did not cause his rabble rousing; he didn't need booze to make a stir.

Mickey fancied himself a knowledgeable food critic, and enjoyed the steadily improving Los Angeles cuisine. Writer Ben Hecht echoed the self-appraisal: "Mickey was a gourmet. Food can make him almost as fretful as the police, especially the wrong kind of ice cream." Yet, detractors like Reid minimized Mickey's culinary tastes. Reid pretended to be shocked that a Jew would eat ham and eggs in public, instead of keeping strictly kosher.

Mickey's close friend, nightlife companion, and constant publicist was Florabel Muir, who wrote for the *New York Daily News* after stints at several major West and East Coast newspapers. The FBI would label Muir "notorious" in their files. The notorious reporter helped define Mickey's career. Journalist Peter Noyes recognized the close bond between Mickey and Muir: "She covered the Sunset Strip beat; she went everywhere with him; she reported on him daily. She was part of the reason that he became a legend."

Mickey became a regular at popular Ciro's, with its wedding-cake-frosted second story and a missing slice. According to author Sheila Weller, he never paid a tab in the legendary nightclub, but was welcome nonetheless at a ringside table.[28]

Juxtaposed to Weller's claim, Mickey was quick to whip out a roll of bills; he was an obscene tipper. To make sure that everyone would remember him, he tipped five and ten dollars, huge sums in the late thirties and early forties. Former boxer Art Aragon recalled in one interview that Mickey was not a ten-dollar tipper, but a regular one-hundred-dollar tipper. "I don't know where he got this money...he bought everybody," said Aragon.

Managers and maître d's, at places like the lavish Coconut Grove inside the Ambassador Hotel, have said that Mickey routinely peeled off a roll of fifties and one hundreds whenever he arrived with his entourage. He loved to pay his way, and three hundred bucks a pop was nothing to him. Headwaiters couldn't wait to see him. Many friends and associates have stated that he went out of his way to take care of everyone's bill, as many as fourteen guests at a time. He never went out alone, and usually had a minimum of eight to ten dinner guests. Writer Dean Jennings knew him to be a "chronic check grabber." Mickey, often seen in the company of mobster actors George Raft and Edward G. Robinson at the Hillcrest Country Club, would leave fifty pairs of shoes for polishing in the men's locker room. Ray Fulce, a locker room attendant from 1956–1959, and now a caddy at the prestigious club, had always marveled at "Mr. Cohen's" generosity. Joe Patti, owner of the former Rat Pack hangout La Famiglia in Beverly Hills, said that Mickey was a very generous tipper, particularly when he was club hopping with beautiful women. When Joe was the bartender at Beverly Hills' other Rat Pack hangout La Scala, non-smoker Mickey gave Joe one of his expensive personal cigarette lighters as a gift.

Mickey had invested in several lawful businesses, prompting the FBI to list his occupation in 1940 as a "gas station owner." Gas-station-owner Mickey was now also the boss of West Coast bookmaking.

He ran an army of muscled employees who helped him rake in millions for Bugsy and the mob. Anytime the FBI came calling, he remained fearless and sarcastic, perhaps accounting for the numerous occupations reported on his records. He had already developed a strong power base, yet some writers who perhaps took "gas station owner" and future occupation listings more literally, labeled him a minor player.

On the social front, LaVonne had been dating Mickey for two years when he arrived with Tuffy (his Boston terrier) and announced immediate marriage plans. Folklore enthusiasts prefer to believe that he was late for most of his dates because of his primping, so he often had one of his bozos pick up LaVonne; he even missed the scheduled time for his wedding.

On October 15, 1940, Tuffy witnessed the middle-of-the-night brief wedding ceremony, despite the minister's complaints. The wedding chapel was located on S. Western Avenue, and the minister maintained affiliations with the Temple of Divine Wisdom. Mickey was twenty-seven and LaVonne twenty-three.

"You can't bring that animal into a wedding!" the minister exclaimed.

Mickey did not acquiesce, and had to rely on LaVonne's charm to persuade the minister. Human witnesses included Mickey stalwarts Joe Sica and Mike Howard.[29] The best man was William "Stumpy" Zevon, who joked with Mickey about the minister's large feet. (Father of future rocker/songwriter Warren Zevon, Stumpy would remain friends with Mickey. On occasion the two men would treat Stumpy's relatives to ice cream on visits to the old Brooklyn neighborhood. During one brief sojourn, an irascible fountain owner made the mistake of not opening up for Mickey and the boys. Mickey changed the owner's mind—some say by merely offering to buy a whole tub of ice cream.)[30]

Mickey's local commitments and growing conflicts over the race wire did not permit a honeymoon. Lavonne's early relationship with him developed during Hollywood's exciting halcyon days, ideal for a young couple on their way up. The Cohens were entrenched in one of the most productive transitions in American business and popular culture, when the entertainment business defined the social lives of locals who had cash to burn.

In keeping with his wife's consistent wishes, Mickey hired a tutor to help with his diction and table manners. His accent and ability to string together sentences improved dramatically. He became more comfortable dining where he bumped into people whose speech implied proper education.

He was hell bent on molding himself into another persona, and fought hard to avoid his character defects. Hollywood gave him all the room to grow out of his brusque, hood's background.

LaVonne grew accustomed to tons of cash and Mickey's peculiar and unscheduled business life. She accepted the double standard; Mickey did whatever he wanted, whenever he wanted, while she led a conventional life, including an overblown conservative profile. She learned to embrace the most prude outlook toward stylish unrefined items like sexy clothing and flashy makeup.

LaVonne knew that his business required him to be out with women, a problem in any marriage. Since the backdrop of the entertainment business and its social Hollywood mores supported risqué behavior, it defined his marriage style. Nobody raised an eyebrow. Like his show business mogul counterparts, seen all over town with starlets, Mickey used women to compliment the schmooze. Mob visitors also expected evening escorts, since social perks usually accompanied deals.

Because of the wire service wars, and the already large number of Mickey enemies, everyone agreed that the army would be a good place for him to hide. As an alternative, the mob had links to protective havens like the Bahamas and parts of the

Caribbean. His attempt to enter the service proved foolhardy.

When he registered on October 16, 1940 (the day after his marriage), the draft board decided he was "morally unfit for military service." They told him that he was already registered 4-F due to a psychiatric examination he had received years back by order of a judge who deemed his courtroom behavior eccentric. Mickey's brother Harry tried to have him reclassified as "of good character and reputation," but the local police would not supply the selective service with enough information to invalidate their negative character description.

Mocambo, the Brazilian-themed club filled with glass-caged macaws, parrots, and cockatoos, opened on January 3, 1941, and had a nearly twenty year run. At the height of the its popularity, Mickey and his strong-arms commanded a ringside table.[31]

One night the famous columnist and Hollywood powerhouse Hedda Hopper noticed that all the guys in Mickey's entourage had bulges, and she was not referring to the legendary Mae West line, "Is that a pickle in your pocket, or are you just glad to see me?" type of bulge.

Hedda saw guns; her response was not phallic. She told the management, "Move him or move me. I won't sit next to this bum." Polite managers escorted Mickey to another table.

While the gang boss was away from his table, likely washing his hands, pal Florabel Muir warned the headstrong Hopper, "You'd better be careful. He'll wipe you out." Muir had a sense of humor; Hopper didn't.

"Wipe me out? He wouldn't dare," Hopper nervously replied.

Walter Winchell took another approach one evening at Ciro's. He, attorney Art Crowley, and private detective Fred Otash, who had a hard-on for Mickey and his delinquents, were dining when Mickey and his entourage arrived, trailed by the Los Angeles Police Department's gangster squad.

Winchell pulled out a gun, slid it across the table to Crowley, and said, "Jesus, with all these different groups in here, there might be some shooting tonight." Otash recalled "nut" Winchell's plan: "Look, if there's any shooting, we'll all duck under the table and start shooting back." Otash didn't say how many guns tough guy Winchell carried.[32]

The FBI believed that Bugsy intended for Mickey to be the next boss, and began a grooming program as early as 1942. Bugsy fancied himself more of a sportsman and personality, and deferred daily business decisions to Mickey, who proved ideal because he had demonstrated his willingness to "kill whenever necessary to get results," an undeniable attribute in his business. Tested employees at his level were scarce. Mickey, despite his independent streak, was still a favorite of the boys back east, and they counted on him to insure a complete takeover.

The FBI account of Mickey's and Bugsy's antics offers a simplistic overview of a more complicated national process. FBI files fill hundreds of pages concerning Mickey's extensive gambling interests, but nobody challenged him. The FBI ignored Lansky's power and control; Lansky pulled all the strings. Bugsy left a lot of the muscle work to Mickey, but no records exist of Mickey's personal participation in hits. He succeeded due to his own persistence, the absence of FBI plans to intercede, excellent attorneys, and corrupt political cooperation. Like one of his lifer employees known only as "Nate S" boasted, "I have been thirty-five years in organized crime—and never a black mark against me." Like Nate, nothing seemed to tarnish Mickey's quest to take over.

Dragna now appeared comfortable with Mickey's takeover of all the gambling. The old-time Italian only wanted to maintain the distribution rights to the Continental Wire Service's racing sheets. Continental's Russell Brophy and James Ragen wanted no part of Mickey. When Dragna met with Bugsy, Mickey, and Joe Sica at a Hollywood drive-in on Sunset and Vermont, he agreed that Mickey was gambling boss and Sica was the narcotics king. Rosselli had already agreed.

In July 1942, as an example of Mickey's early contributions to securing the race wire service, he and Joe Sica beat up non-cooperative rival Russell Brophy. The brutes tore out the telephones and hit him on the head with a gun. He complained to the police. Sica paid a $200 fine to Mickey's $100; the erroneous charge of murder having been reduced to a simple assault.

"I guess I only beat him a hundred bucks worth," was Mickey's quip years later.

Through Mickey's strong-arm antics, all the local bookies begrudgingly acquiesced to the national reorganization, and Mickey and Bugsy took further control out West. The war of the wire services had also taken its toll nationally, and most small-time operators no longer cared whom they were associated with, as long as no business interruptions occurred. One by one, the bookies fell into line when muscled by the new race wire syndicate, and the country was poised to offer expanded national betting services.

Even though Mickey did not serve his country, there was more illegal work at home because of the war. A secondary market developed around ration stamps and any item that was in short supply provided an excellent opportunity for the racketeers, in effect creating a "black market" in the U.S. They jumped on the swag, and sold everything they could get their hands on. Mickey entered the black market as soon as World War II started. He made a ton of money; it was easy for him. Rationed food items included butter, sugar, coffee, chocolate, and red meat—all to help accommodate the troops. The government set the standards for basic food requirements and issued rationing stamp booklets. Even infants had to be registered. Tires and gasoline were always in short supply.

The mob stumbled into a ready-made business. The syndicate saw to it that these items were always available at a premium, and often insisted that a customer buy some extra bootleg booze along with his purchase of staples. One of the largest secondary markets was nylon products, which made stockings a hot item. Even before the war broke out, silk imports from Japan had stopped. The War Production Board controlled silk supplies in America, and commandeered what was already in short supply for parachutes. This set off a run by women on the remaining silk stockings, and an instant black market item that everyone demanded. A male suitor or apologetic husband could do no wrong with flowers and a pair of silk stockings. The government eventually stopped DuPont from manufacturing any nylon stockings. It was another gold mine for the syndicate, and the boys cornered the market.

The Cohens would move several times in the early years of their marriage in order to accommodate Mickey's growing wardrobe, as well as his passion for more luxurious accommodations. Until 1942, he maintained a residence in Burbank, a city that would become a consistent source of revenue. During the mid-forties, he lived at 9938½ Robbins Drive in Beverly Hills, adjacent to the central restaurant and shopping area, and later in tony Brentwood. One of his main offices was located at 141½ North La Brea Avenue, a few miles east of Beverly Hills, and close to the Strip.

The upscale moves resulted in another naïve FBI report: "Cohen had attracted the attention of the No. 1 Gang Lord in Los Angeles, Benjamin (Bugsie) [sic] Siegel, and as a result of their association he was soon able to move into more pretentious quarters in Los Angeles." The in-denial FBI acted as if Mickey and Bugsy operated independently. Even though Mickey contended that he was standoffish in the beginning of their relationship, both men had to answer to Lansky. Organized crime was already nationally controlled, and modeled on American corporate structure. Lansky would one day boast, "We're bigger than U.S. Steel."

Mickey enjoyed his Beverly Hills digs, and the protection that the insulated city afforded him. New Beverly Hills police chief Clinton Anderson made it difficult for any driver to stop a car for five minutes after midnight. The fervent night patrols proved successful, and made it tough for any outside criminals to hang around Beverly Hills after hours.

Chief Anderson appeared impressed when he described the affluent neighborhood:

> White-pillared Colonials, tile-roofed Spanish homes in pinks and blues, glass-walled moderns and low-slung ranch houses border winding streets lined by palm trees 60 feet in height...artificial waterfalls, indoor fountains, private trout pools, inlaid marble floors transported from European castles...gold-plated bathroom fixtures and private motion-picture projection booths for home screenings.

It was also a nice environment for mobsters to socialize. Thanks to the police, Mickey had less fear of a hit in Beverly Hills, and became a regular in the little burgeoning city's nightclubs and restaurants.

LaVonne was not immune to Mickey's way of life; she lived in constant fear of his demise, and a normal family life was out of the question. He and LaVonne had planned for children, and eventually considered an adoption. Mickey vetoed it, citing problems once the war had begun. He knew he couldn't provide a proper life for a child.

One night he instructed LaVonne to pick him up after a card game. She couldn't find him until midnight, staggering down the street with his hands supporting his head with newspapers to stop the bleeding. Someone at the game had hit Mickey on the head with an iron pipe, and he was able to escape the card room by jumping out of a window.

Another time he arrived home to the sound of machine guns. Still in his car, he sped away, while she anxiously called all over town, and finally located her beloved at Neddie Herbert's, a former New Yorker and close confidant of Mickey's.

LaVonne once told Florabel Muir, while sitting with Mickey in the breakfast room,

> I wonder what it would be like to sit in a room with the lights on and all the shades up. I drive past other people's homes and see them sitting there in front of their windows not worrying about somebody shooting at them.

Mickey complained, often in the form of teasing: "That's why I wish I'd never got married..."

LaVonne pinched Mickey's ear and chirped, "You wouldn't be alive if it weren't for me looking out for you. You don't need to worry about me..."

In 1943, the frustrated authorities finally took on the mob in court. The sensational Hollywood Extortion Case took seventy-three days and resulted in multiple guilty verdicts. The Hollywood unions, including the Stage Handlers Union and the Movie Projectionist Union, had had enough members to entice the Chicago mob to take control. Frank Nitti and Paul Ricca were able to extort large sums of money from MGM, Paramount, Twentieth Century Fox, Columbia, and RKO. On March 19, after Willie Bioff and George Browne had ratted him out, Nitti shot himself in the head. Rosselli would serve three years in Leavenworth prison. The case proved to be an isolated attempt to control the West Coast mob.

Mickey's business profits escalated, payrolls increased, and cash flowed from the illicit faucets. Several of his hoods made $1100 per week. Neddie Herbert was at the top, and with good reason. FBI files listed him as an ex-killer who worked for Bugsy. He was always much closer to Mickey, and some report that Mickey grew up with him. Neddie never impressed journalists as the murder-for-hire type. Most found him funny, although he was mechanically proficient with a machine gun.

"He could take a machine gun apart and put it together again in record time, better than any U.S. Marine expert's time. And he was also a crack shot with the same type of weapon," was Mickey's proud take on Neddie's skill.

Neddie was fearless; he once spit into the face of mob leader Joe Adonis. The verdict of the syndicate Round Table in New York was humiliation; Neddie's own brothers would beat him to even the score. He loved animals, and once shared his New York apartment with a gorilla. The boys called Neddie "a card"; he kept them in stitches. He always substituted the word "prostituter" for "prosecutor." Anytime Mickey finished squeezing into his third tightly fitting pastel suit of the day, Neddie would look him over, feign hunger, and ask, "Hey, Mickey, you got an orange on you?" Neddie was a man with a unique and fearless sense of humor—Mickey's court jester. He was always on Mickey's side, and remained second in command while providing comic relief like any good sidekick.

Other employees garnered five hundred per week. The lowest rung on the payroll was two hundred—plus all they could steal. The FBI was aware of the unreported cash changing hands, but did not interfere.

Mickey made the most of Hollywood's ability to pamper its citizens; he took advantage of his shopping opportunities, and continued to fill his obscenely vast wardrobe, which was essential to his approach to work. He, who always wore new suits and ties (sometimes never wearing the same suit twice), was a regular at Bullock's Wilshire department store. He liked to mingle with the wealthy Jewish shoppers, purchasing the fanciest items in town despite the outrageous cost of imported goods. He thought nothing of shelling out three hundred bucks for a Panama hat. He was conscious of which gangsters dressed the best, like fashion plates Frank Costello, Luciano, and Bugsy. (Bugsy always wore cashmere suits, something Mickey didn't like for himself; cashmere wrinkled too easily, and he wanted to have a clear crease in his trousers.)

Mickey's view of his trappings was simple: "If you can't live well, you might as well be out of it altogether, you know what I mean?" He wanted all the nice material things that went with success.

He and Bugsy liked to have their hair cut at Gornik and Drucker's in Beverly Hills.[33] Columnist Steve Harvey relates that founder Harry Drucker became concerned when rival gangs started hanging around at the same time. The manager alerted Drucker that customers were afraid to visit, and feared that the adversaries would shoot it out like in the gangster movies. That never happened, and mob influence in Beverly Hills continued.

Mickey realized early on that the fancy cars and clothing did not entirely make the man. He was still crude, a rough character, and he knew that it put some people off. He couldn't accept that and craved assimilation with people he considered to be of a "higher element." He didn't see himself as gangster, but rather an entrepreneur.

Some upper-echelon mobsters echoed his feelings and encouraged him to stay away from the violent end of the business. Many of the Jewish mobsters already had established themselves in legitimate businesses, and paved the way for their descendants to lead respectable lives, like the bootlegger Bronfmans[34] and race wire Annenbergs.[35] Even Frank Costello had suggested a legit life to Mickey, and now Bugsy whispered in his ear about diversifying his regular business investments. He obliged and began to buy up real estate on the Strip, increase his splits in fancy supper clubs, and establish more ventures for the East Coast mob.

In the process, he became a constant fixture on the Strip's social scene, one that now existed only with his and Bugsy's imprimatur, since their influence had infiltrated all the top clubs. He furiously made the rounds at night, hell bent on establishing himself as a Hollywood celebrity by hobnobbing with the rich. Social climber Mickey would develop long-standing friendships with Robert Mitchum, Sammy Davis, Jr., Errol Flynn, and Ben Hecht. The future Rat Pack needed a place to play, and he helped provide it. Without him, perhaps the Rat Pack phenomenon never would have happened. Despite his character and reputation, he had no problem fitting in with the Rat-Packers-in-training and their business and social entourage. Entertainers loved the mob—where else could they gamble in the days before Vegas?

The higher ups on both sides of the legal divide had one thing in common—they wanted to attend black tie dinners with famous producers and beautiful actresses. Just as Mickey had, national politicians and corporations courted Hollywood for its ability to sway public thinking. Washington and Hollywood have always made strange alliances, and created a growing web that connected show business, organized crime, and politics.

The Golden Age theatrics of the Los Angeles mob had arrived; the opening act of the Mickey and Bugsy Show was a hit. Without them, organized crime could never have developed so swiftly around Hollywood. This network would continue for decades. The national mob set the stage for the big move to Las Vegas. Showstoppers, a series of macabre events that even the best playwrights could not have imagined, filled the remainder of the production.

3.

Mickey combined his burning desire for social acceptance with the nuts-and-bolts of running a growing organized business, while becoming the first in his profession to develop a crafty public image. "If you lived in L.A. in the forties and you didn't know who Mickey Cohen was you had to be in a mental institution. He was everyone's ideal of a gangster, in this town," boasted journalist Peter Noyes.

Mickey's varied business interests soared, supplying him with an enormous cash flow to support his flamboyant lifestyle. He remained beholden to higher ups like Lansky, who supervised the growth of a tiered corporate syndicate. While the pint-sized entrepreneur was always tempted to make money in legitimate businesses—he now owned several—crime proved his only consistent and reliable means of income.

He controlled most of the gambling in Los Angeles. The national syndicate knew that he could immediately lay off bets of between fifty and one hundred thousand dollars. Americans loved to gamble, and were ready to bet off track at a moment's notice, a phenomenon that solidified his position. "For every person that went to the track there was a hundred that went to the bookies," noted crime historian James Johnston. Mickey's casino and bookie interests expanded further, thanks to a blossoming following of movie stars and rich locals. His early experiences with bookmaking helped him establish a pervasive syndicate throughout greater Los Angeles. "Nothing went unless I O.K.'d it," were his own words.

Cash also spilled from businesses tied to public consumption. He provided protection for large operations, owned and distributed cigarette vending machines, resold stolen liquor, and sold drugs. Nothing was off limits, so long as it brought in money, and some appeared very legitimate. In 1944, Mickey's pal Charlie Shuster, who fronted for him as a fight promoter,[1] built the first commercial building near the Los Angeles Airport, a Jim Dandy Market in Westchester.[2] Many suspected that Shuster's chain of supermarkets was a front for gambling operations. While money laundering and stolen goods, particularly during the wartime rationing, were associated with illegal fronts of this type, authorities never linked either to Jim Dandy.

Despite favorable accounts written by sympathetic journalists, some employed by Mickey, he was indeed involved in narcotics. Mexico provided a steady flow of drugs into California, under the auspices of Bugsy and Mickey. The supply lines were originally organized and managed through Al Capone's reign.

Gary Wean, an L.A.P.D. detective sergeant and later a Criminal Intelligence Investigator for the L. A. district attorney, often tailed Mickey around town. One night the first stop was the Pink Pagoda in Chinatown's tourist trap. He later met with bondsman pal Abe Phillips and legal beagle Harry Pregerson at the South Gate Arena. They all ended up at another Chinese joint, Tangs, near City Hall. Mickey dropped off a man in Chinatown named Abe Davidian, who was tracked down by police, and found heading north with millions of dollars worth of narcotics. Davidian would never testify in court because he was found shot to death before the trial.[3]

Mickey's social life rivaled that of any celebrity entertainer, a combination that allowed him to continue nurturing his playground for junior Rat Packers and their coterie, while he mingled regularly with the entertainment power base. His contribution was always making a market in prostitution; one employee source was his Hollywood talent agencies that maintained rosters of young people from all over the country.⁴ Sex for gangsters was a given, an intrinsic recreation and concomitant venerable form of illicit revenue. Mickey made the most of his free social time, and combined the latter financial aspect of sex with pleasure. In May of 1944, the FBI surveillance teams watched him and his boys set up "a large seven-room mansion located at 9100 Hazen," today home to actor Hal Holbrook, with neighbors *Dynasty*'s Linda Evans and *Star Trek*'s Jonathan Frankes. The FBI made no effort to interfere with the luxurious brothel on Hazen. The Feds felt that the responsibility lay with the local authorities, many of whom benefited from Mickey's sexy playground establishments.

Soon completed, the fancy joint was a spectacular party house where a special list of Mickey's friends could spend the night in "wild all-night orgies, and party-girl bouts." The FBI further described the location as a meeting place for "Hollywood personalities." While popular Mickey was host of "commercial sex parties" catering to the rich and famous, what many of the celebrities didn't know was that he would never hesitate to use his knowledge of anyone's sex life for extortion and blackmail; candid movie footage and snapshots materialized as needed. The Hazen house was Mickey's private sexual sound stage.

He once told Ben Hecht, "I never entered a whore house, except to heist it." Hecht never shared Mickey's purported lascivious reputation: "The Jew Boy was not only virginal toward sex, but also toward booze, tobacco, and drugs." He felt that violence delighted Mickey more than sex. By his own admission later in life, Mickey concurred: "To tell the truth, I don't go for it much... Girls very often like me and seem attracted to me, and I find them also attractive, at times."

Despite his later contrition, he still bragged that during his tenure in Los Angeles he had sex two to three times a day. A steady flow of striking actresses, models, and professional ladies dined regularly with sociable Mickey, more likely for his power and growing celebrity, than for his debatable carnal prowess.

By 1945, Bugsy raked in over $25,000 a month, mostly thanks to Mickey, who in addition to controlling the basic gambling had a leg up in the important race wire. With all the illegal gambling action and maneuvers into legitimate business, the authorities occasionally had to make it seem that they were trying to fight organized crime, but the grandstanding efforts were minimal. Los Angeles appeared resigned to accept its criminal partners, this despite the scrutiny of John Hansen, head of the L.A.'s FBI.

The top brass in Cleveland had told Mickey that it was necessary for him to participate in the developing Las Vegas project. He and Bugsy often traveled to Vegas, while most of the gambling action at the time was in Reno. The wartime economy brought in defense workers and soldiers—hardly the high rollers. Occasionally, some flamboyant visitors dropped between $700 and $1400 during their stay.

Bugsy and his partners Gus Greenbaum and Moe Sedway (Morris Sidwirtz) bought the El Cortez Hotel from Marion Hicks, and promptly sold it for a profit of nearly $200,000.[5]

Greenbaum was a successful Arizona bookie, who would prove to have a knack for managing casinos. During one meeting, he beat up Mickey. "Greenbaum reached across the table and grabbed Cohen by the tie and began to kick him under the table...until his shins bled...he gave a shove and Cohen's chair flew back, spilling the little mobster on the floor." According to Mickey bashers, Moe Sedway witnessed the event, and he and Greenbaum resumed their conversation while Mickey limped away.

The initial visits to Vegas by Mickey and Bugsy were to make certain that the new Trans America wire service, headquartered in Phoenix, ran properly; it was essential for the entire Vegas operation. This vast company leased 23,000 miles of telegraph circuits from Western Union, and cost the syndicate $1,000,000 per year. Moses Annenberg, who had worked as a circulation manager for Hearst newspapers, under pressure from the federal authorities—income tax fraud—had given up his own Nationwide wire service in 1939, and paved the way for the smooth operation of third competitor Continental. Al Capone was ultimately not very happy with Annenberg's operation, and likely influenced his decision to quit; Annenberg feared for his life.

Many people close to Bugsy have said that he actually hated the desert, and despised having to spend so much time in Nevada. Mickey was no tagalong either when it came to heat and sand; he thought Vegas was a lark, and wanted nothing to do with it. Despite his distaste for Las Vegas, he regularly accompanied Bugsy on the desert trips. His bookmaking business was a cash machine, and he was pleased to focus on that.

Mickey's favorite and only hotel in the underdeveloped desert was the El Rancho Vegas. The other small hotels and properties away from the strip offered him few of the amenities he needed. He liked to reside in one of the hotel's casitas. The only problem was the trek from the little bungalow to the main building. Since he always liked to show off his wardrobe, he unhappily risked dirtying his fancy duds in Vegas windstorms.[6]

Mickey commented on his dislike for the new venue: "Vegas and I disagreed, so I had to push myself to go there." He had no reason to suspect better times ahead, but he cooperated with the Jewish Desert Storm. He, self-admittedly, could not have been more wrong about the potential of Las Vegas. Many in both the Italian and Jewish mobs had shared his initial opinion. On the other side were visionaries to fuel the phenomenon. Examples included Roger Leonard ("Kallman de Leonard"), a pal of Mickey's and Joe Sica. Leonard and Sica insisted that they get in on the Vegas operation.

During the period of the Vegas jaunts, Mickey introduced new friend Frank Sinatra, who always called Mickey "Michael," to James Tarantino. Sinatra was building his close social coterie, which the newspapers then called the Varsity, the forerunner of the Rat Pack.[7] Tarantino wanted to publish a scandal sheet, *Hollywood Nite Life,* to blackmail celebrities. He immediately became part of Sinatra's group. Sinatra gave him $15,000 to set up the magazine; Mickey had pressured him personally, and extracted $5,000 from him on three separate occasions.[8]

Bobby Garcia, who ran the Cover in Palm Springs, an illegal club frequented by Sinatra, commented on his customer's new pal: "Frank was so enthused about meeting Mickey Cohen, the big shot of the underworld." Garcia warned Sinatra: "They are going to keep five-thousanding you to death, you stupid son of a bitch. I'll tell you what I'll do. I'll tear up your marker if you quit gambling." Garcia claimed that Sinatra reformed after that.

Anytime after that when Tarantino was short of cash, he came to Mickey, who knew about all the proposed articles and offered editorial opinions. He always represented that he had protected his Hollywood friends from the scandal tabloid. He threatened Tarantino after he published negative press on Louella Parsons, someone who took every opportunity to mention Mickey in her gossip column. Later, after a tiff over a proposed series of critical articles on Judy Garland, including her drug use, Mickey claimed that he was instrumental in shutting down *Hollywood Nite Life*.

His power and notoriety attracted more unlikely liaisons, and he began a perverse relationship with Richard Nixon, one that lasted a lifetime. Early in his career, Nixon began taking money from Mickey.

"I always had a bad feeling about Nixon, though," Mickey revealed years later.

On the surface, the relationship might appear to be a strange match, a social system gone awry: why would a Southern California boy like Nixon want anything to do with a Brooklyn-born hood? One of the few things they had in common was their published year of birth, 1913.

Late in 1945, Republican leaders chose Nixon to run for representative from the Twelfth District against popular New Deal Democrat Jerry Voorhis. Nixon knew he would lose the election without Mickey's help and imprimatur: Los Angeles was a Mickey stronghold; he controlled the territory that Nixon sought. Ambitious Nixon had no interest in returning to law practice in provincial Whittier. In order to run for the House seat, he surrounded himself with local powerhouses. To ensure Mickey's backing, he wisely asked for a meeting.

Author Anthony Summers described the somewhat clandestine meeting: "It took place, Cohen said, at Goodfellow's Grotto, a little fish house where the politicians met and where they pull the screens across the booths for these kinds of talks... The meeting was arranged by Murray Chotiner." Chubby, cigar-chomping Chotiner was an attorney who liked his silk ties, monogrammed shirts, and jeweled accessories.

Mickey's other recollections were more casual and slightly different:

> I first met Nixon when he started running for Congress in 1945. It was a matter of one situation

leading into another. Like somebody would say, "Well, ya ought to get together with Dick," or "Ya ought to know Dick."

The little politician even recalled a contradictory venue:

> He [Nixon] was just starting to get his foot into the door, and Orange County where he was from was important to my bookmaking program. I met Nixon there in a coffee shop. I think all I really said to him was something like "We got some ideas, we may put some things in motion."

Nixon cared very little about bookmaking or Mickey's criminal activities; his aspirations were more grandiose. Mickey's interest in politics at the local level wasn't very complicated—he was always looking for another politician to put on his payroll.

Mickey could not have done a better job for any politician.

> For his campaign I gave a $5,000 check which I used to have a copy of. My friend Myford Irvine of the Irvine ranch family was my man in Orange County on certain propositions. The contribution was important for me and for the country. It was also Irvine's wishes. Irvine was powerful, as far as

he was instrumental and a part and parcel of me running out there, so when he asked, I gave. In fact I think a bigger amount was asked, but I Jewed him down to $5,000.[9]

The FBI knew about Mickey and his new pal Nixon, but had a policy that precluded any intervention: "It was diplomatically, but very firmly, re-emphasized...that the Bureau would not become a party to political activities in any form..."

Nixon told a cheering crowd during the Voorhis election, "I want you to know that I am your candidate primarily because there are no special strings attached to me. I have no support from any special interest or pressure group." Nixon ran a dirty smear campaign, called Voorhis a Communist, won the election, and remained friends with Mickey. Their paths crossed many times.

Rowland Evans, Jr., and Robert D. Novak shed some light on why Nixon played ball with Mickey. "Richard Nixon's personal reputation was that of a hard man, bordering on meanness." A common ground existed for conducting business. Mickey and many mobsters shared Nixon's ill temper and skill as a master at manipulating mass communications. "He [Nixon] was always a man alone," understood biographer Richard Reeves. So was Mickey.

When back in Hollywood, sometimes a bullet was necessary to reinforce business interests. Mickey's description of his relationship with the competitive Shaman brothers was graphic. He didn't like them because "they thought they were real tough." He felt that the Shamans were insignificant talent, part of the hoards of lower strata criminals he had to step over after moving west.

On Monday, May 14, 1945, Mickey beat up Max Shaman's older brother Joe at the newly opened La Brea Social Club. According to Mickey, he wasn't responsible for the fight with the Shaman boy, who was disturbing the peace in the restaurant. "So Hooky broke a chair over his head and bodily threw him out of the joint—slapped the shit of him, you know, gave him a deal, gave him a going over." The La Brea Social Club was a well-known Hollywood hangout that featured a fancy craps table above the home-style restaurant. Actor George Raft had given Mickey $100,000 to invest in the club.[10] Hooky Rothman, Mickey's lifelong friend, helped run the elaborate La Brea Club setting, while host Mickey enjoyed the fruits of his most recent labor. The customer base featured gambling pros like Nick the Greek and Sacramento Butch. The upstairs area handled everything illegal, including sports betting. Mickey was boastful of his housekeeper's cooking talents; she even baked on the premises. He understood his restaurant didn't rival the new Chasen's restaurant, which he referred to as "gourmet cooking," but it was popular nevertheless.[11]

The next day Shaman brothers Max and Izzy announced that they were going to give Mickey "the beating of his life." They advertised their intentions by searching for Mickey at his La Brea Social Club and Santa Anita Park. Mickey also operated a paint store, actually a gambling front, at 8109 Beverly Boulevard; it stocked as many scratch sheets, racing forms, and bookie junk as it did paint supplies. Izzy waited in the car while Max checked the store. Izzy heard shots, ran to the door, and heeded warnings not to enter. Then he heard three or four more shots and ran back to his car for his own gun.

That Tuesday afternoon, when twenty-eight-year-old Max Shaman had come in screaming, Mickey—as they whispered in the gangster movies—already had the drop on him. He always kept a pistol on or in the desk and fired before Shaman could pull the trigger on his own gun. The featherweight bookie had shot Max Shaman to death with a thirty-eight. When Izzy returned he found Max dead. Since Mickey was the only one in the store, he had to confess to police. The authorities marked off the confrontation as revenge.

Estes Kefauver, chairman of the Senate Committee on Organized Crime, wrote extensively on his interviews with Mickey, and referenced his menacing past. Kefauver's version of the entire Shaman incident conflicts directly with Mickey's; however Mickey did corroborate the shooting. He explained to Kefauver:

> ...he reaches toward me with a gun. He was going to shoot me. So that was it. I blew my top. You gotta remember, I was different than I am now. I was a wild-haired kid. I blasted him with a piece I had in my desk.

For legal help after the Shaman shooting, he turned to reliable attorney Jerry Geisler, who told Mickey to get him $25,000 right away and he would take care of everything. Geisler received the money that night. Frank Costello sent an extra $100,000 to Los Angeles to ensure Mickey's fair treatment.
The coroner's jury inquest insisted that police hold Mickey for murder.
In court, he flatly stated, "I shot in self-defense, Your Honor."
District Attorney Fred Napoleon Howser, who replaced deceased John Dockweiler, part of the Artie Samish political machine, was easily convinced of Mickey's innocence.[12] His 1944 appointment

materialized under suspicious circumstances: the Board of Supervisors approved him before the public had any inkling, or the proper burial of Howser's predecessor had taken place.

After a private court conference with Geisler, Assistant District Attorney William E. Simpson agreed that Mickey acted in self-defense, "protecting himself from bodily assault by a larger man." Six-foot Max Shaman weighed 230 pounds to Mickey's undersized five-three, only 145 pounds.

The judge accepted Mickey's self-defense plea, "justifiable homicide," dropped the charges, and dismissed the case. His arrest is not on the record.

Mickey knew that the Shaman killing left many people unhappy. He told reporters that mysterious cars had begun following him and cruising around his Robbins Drive home. To satisfy him, police investigated and sent protection, headed by Detective Lieutenant L. R. Veit. Mickey made sure that reporters printed that he was leaving for a month's vacation.

The police raided the La Brea Club twice in November 1945, the first time with twenty arrests. On November 20, police arrested the "31-year-old Hollywood sporting figure" and twelve other men. They held Mickey briefly on felony charges related to robbery and guns found at the location. The police admitted that the raid was an ordinary "vice shakedown," forcing the Deputy District Attorney Don Avery to refuse the complaint.

Mickey was now as prominent as Bugsy in Los Angeles. His bad-boy status was firmly elevated to the national level. He developed entire geographical areas, almost at will. He found a significant weak spot in the policing of the San Fernando Valley, an expansive underdeveloped area north of Beverly Hills. The soft city beyond the Canyons was Burbank, where he had resided.[13]

Mickey set up a gambling operation on a horse farm called the Dincara Stock Farm, at 806 S. Mariposa Street, now part of artsy NoHo (North of Hollywood). He had craps, chemin de fer, blackjack, and slots. He gave away food and drink, something casinos would learn to do when the legalized gambling business grew. He employed a string of Filipino houseboys whose number rivaled the roster of his equestrian stables. Service was first class, and so were the customers.

He boasted, "It was the goddamdest joint you ever seen. You'd come in there in the afternoon and you'd think you was on a movie set, because there was everybody from Warner Brothers and other studios." Actors still in their soldier or cowboy outfits headed in for lunch, sometimes just to "kibitz with the guys around there."

He led the life of an English squire. He learned to ride, complete with the fanciest garb, including the shiny boots, and hobnobbed with the society set that preferred English to Western riding. Mickey, by his own admission, was a fish out of water, with his crude Brownsville/Boyle Heights mouth, spewing profanities from up on his horse, decked to the nines like a British gentleman. He visited friends in his new outfit, always arriving with gifts, such as French pastries. The rich ladies found him amusing, and he rode alongside them with funnyman Neddie Herbert.

The police ignored his Burbank takeover. He had a key man inside the department, and paid huge sums to keep the force in tow. He paid the higher-ranking officials $1000 per month. He also hired Blanie Matthews, the chief of police at Warner Brothers Studios. Jack Dineen, a retired police captain, oversaw Mickey's entire operation. The FBI rightly blamed the local police cooperation for Mickey's success. He confessed, "My horses was an operation which I done for my own personal entertainment. But you realize that none of these things would operate for five minutes if it wasn't for the cooperation of the powers." Even with multiple raids on the ranch in the late forties, the gambling joint would reopen.

On January 10, 1946, over three inches of snow uncharacteristically stalled the city of Burbank and the surrounding ranches and orchards. The extremely rare weather served as a natural metaphor whilst a white blanket covered the soiled city, whose slogan, "People, Pride, and Progress," should have included gambling, movies, and Mickey Cohen.

Police harassed him regularly in Beverly Hills and Hollywood. When private detective Fred Otash had worked for the police department, his regular orders had included rousting Mickey. "When I was a cop our orders were to get Mickey Cohen on anything we could. I went after him tenaciously." He would later work for Mickey and supply him with "lawyers with facts that made him look good."

Future nemesis vice squad Officer Rudy Wellpott and partner J. G. Fisk picked Mickey up at his club on North La Brea Avenue. This time the officers dug up the old 1934 embezzlement charge from Cleveland, and arrested him for not registering as an ex-convict. The papers again referred to him as a "Hollywood sporting figure." Attorney Sam Rummel filed a demurrer—a claim of insufficient legal basis—against the petty January 31, 1946, arrest. Mickey was back in action quickly after posting a $500 bond.

Even with extra police protection and tails, on March 15 someone robbed Mickey's apartment of over $10,000 in furs and jewelry. The FBI surmised that he had his wife's things stolen because he was short on cash. He refused to sign a complaint with the Beverly Hills Police Department, and they dropped the matter.

During 1946 Mickey became acquainted with Jack Ruby (Rubenstein), who years later would kill JFK's assassin Lee Harvey Oswald. Then a Los Angeles detective, author Gary Wean still followed Mickey all over town. He has written extensively about the connection between the former Jack Rubinstein and Mickey. Unsavory Ruby, who started out as a punchboard-gambling salesman, led a degenerate life. He liked to brag about his contacts with the mob, and one of the names he mentioned most often when he tried to impress someone was Mickey, who was one of his idols.

Wean first encountered Ruby inside Mickey's black limousine; Mickey's boys chauffeured Ruby all over town.

I was working University Division. The Inglewood Police Department would hire off-duty L.A.P.D. officers to help them direct the heavy traffic to the Hollywood Race Track. It was there

I became acquainted with Mickey Cohen and his hoodlum friend, Jack Ruby, from Chicago.

Through Mickey, crime voyeur Ruby was privy to the developments of the West Coast operations. His eventual rise to power thoroughly impressed Ruby, who was already enamored of Mickey's associations with Hollywood moguls and movie stars.

Wean observed that Mickey "had several talks with Jack Ruby who was managing Harry's Place on Main Street." Ruby and Mickey would hang out at Harry's and another location named the Red Devil.

The years 1946–47 saw the elimination of many Mickey rivals. The *Evening Herald* reported that "...two men in a swift black car" killed major bookmaker Pauley Gibbons as he returned to his Beverly Hills apartment at 116 North Gale Drive."

It was 2:30 a.m. on May 2, 1946. The forty-five-year-old Gibbons, who had thirty arrests to his credit, bit the dust. Seven bullets felled him, and he yelled from the sidewalk, "Don't kill me! Please don't kill me! Help! Help!" as nervous neighbors peered through curtains. The assailants had waited near Wilshire and Gale until they spotted him. Earlier that evening, he had asked his brother Myer for money. Myer promised to help, but not soon enough. Gibbons wore a gold diamond sapphire ring and a gold watch at the time of his death. The assassins removed neither.

Beverly Hills Police Chief Anderson said that he could have easily supplied a dozen motives for the murder. Police questioned liquor storeowner Harold Marks, who had previously threatened Gibbons for welshing on a gambling debt. Marks also owned the Fair-Bev club where Gibbons played cards, and did so just before his death.

Months later Gibbons' partners Benny "The Meatball" Gamson, a suspect in Gibbons' own death, and George Levinson, "his torpedo," were also knocked off while inside their Beverly Boulevard residence on October 3, 1946. Gamson was bestowed his less-than-flattering moniker because he looked like a meatball on spindly legs. The *Evening Herald* referred to him as the current "No. 1 bookie." *Life* humorously reported that he died of an occupational disease—"gunfire."

Gamson's death netted Mickey 10,000 new bookies. By then he was taking in over $80,000 per week in protection money alone. The FBI suspected that he was behind the Gibbons hit, as well as others. Everyone who was a threat to his eventual rise disappeared.

After years of conflict with Mickey in Los Angeles, Dragna acquiesced to muscling in on the local Vegas bookmakers. He provided the armor that controlled the fledgling Vegas hotel operations, then nothing more than mom-and-pop motels with gambling. The Vegas activity only angered Dragna, since Bugsy and Mickey excluded him from the detailed talks about expansion. He was already disappointed with the Bugsy-Mickey takeover of the West Coast and Los Angeles, and was less excited about his new role as the muscle to pave the way into Vegas. Regardless of the friction, Dragna helped eliminate local competition in order to perpetuate a national gambling syndicate.

The Vegas operation now needed firmer control of the wire service in order to succeed. Bookies paid the service up to $1200 per week for the gambling information. James Ragen, national head of Continental Press Service, was one of the first competitors to feel the pressure of elimination. He knew he couldn't last, even though Dragna and Rosselli backed the Continental.[14] Ragen, whose son-in-law Russell Brophy had taken the beating from Mickey, spoke with the Chicago FBI agents, and hoped for protection. He pushed for Capone's old Chicago mob-backed Trans America, as agreed at the national level. Bugsy, Mickey, and Joe Sica were the strong-arm, and all focused on one goal: get control of the wire.

Senator Estes Kefauver considered the Continental Press wire service "Public Enemy

Number One," and knew that the wire service ensured continuous Vegas business for the mob. Yet, he appeared somewhat naïve when he painted a picture of the then current state of criminal affairs:

> When the "noble experiment" [Prohibition] ended, the gangs had to look for a new and equally lucrative racket. Organized prostitution had already been made difficult by passage of the Mann [White Slave] Act. Narcotics was profitable but definitely limited as an operation of universal appeal.

The Los Angeles office of the FBI bugged Mickey's home beginning May 24, 1946, and periodically attempted to bug his offices. The surveillance was particularly unsuccessful regarding the syndicate's elaborate Vegas plans; nothing turned up about the wire wars either. The new bugs were part of a program entitled "Reactivation of the Capone Gang," and included Bugsy and Dragna.

On June 24, Harry "Red" Richmond, a Chicago bookie, was gunned down in front of his home after switching back to Continental.

Eleven days later James Ragen barely escaped a drive-by shooting, which included a fifteen-mile, sixty-miles-per-hour chase. The Chicago police gave him protection only after he ran into a precinct.

An old beat-up delivery truck loaded with orange crates turned out to be the next hit vehicle. Two gunmen flipped the tarpaulin and opened fire on Ragen. One record indicates that he may have died from mercury poisoning, rather than his multiple shotgun wounds received on August 14, 1946. Mickey and Bugsy had likely set up the Ragen hit to the chagrin of Rosselli and Dragna.

The competition had become a prestige issue with Dragna, who took out his frustrations on Mickey, and targeted him for hits. Prospective assassins turned down offers flat, like one to Mocambo-robber Robert Savirino, who told police that his offer to bump off Mickey was a paltry $2,500 and not worth the risk. More attempts to get Mickey loomed on the horizon.

When all the dust settled, the wire was in place, headed on the West Coast by Bugsy and Mickey.

Bugsy was obsessed with Las Vegas and had Lansky's approval. He envisioned—but not quite the same way as depicted in the movies—the potential in the desert, and perceived that Beverly Hills residents were an easy mark for cash on junkets there. Popular culture has extensively explored the folklore surrounding the discovery of Las Vegas. Bugsy, obviously overtaken by the desert sun, stands in barren sand dunes and spiritually envisions a casino. Actor Warren Beatty, portraying

Bugsy in the movie, shouts, "I got it! I got it! It came to me like a vision! Like a religious epiphany." Witness Harvey Keitel (as Mickey) wonders if Bugsy is speaking about God. At least critic Peter Travers inserted a jab regarding the historical inaccuracy and sentimentality of *Bugsy*: "Siegel had vision. At least this movie thinks so."[15]

Insiders knew that Bugsy did not have the temperament or creative initiative to have come up with the Flamingo Club idea on his own, nor did his harsh management style fit the proposed image of the casino. Mickey identified the personality defect, and warned him, "In the East, people are kind of abrupt and brusque, particularly in the racket world, but you don't do that out here." He had learned to tone down his East Coast gangster moxie when it came to corporate business.

It was Lansky's idea to place Bugsy into a project that had already begun; Bugsy was not present at the inception of the Flamingo. The new bandwagon was composed of an ensemble of creative criminals and the best available companies in corporate America. It was not smooth going; problems continually cropped up, from the simple objective kind involved with building to the intervention of many powerful personalities.

Dragna's own attempt to shake Lansky down for a piece of the Flamingo ended with a whimper.

Jimmy "The Weasel" Fratianno reported that Lansky asked Dragna to come up with $125,000 for a piece of the action. Lansky knew that was out of his league and the request wouldn't materialize a second time. Dragna proved again to be an ineffectual leader, never truly feared, and therefore unable to control future activities in California and Las Vegas.

To build the Flamingo Club ("Flamingo" was his girlfriend Virginia Hill's nickname, after her deep throat fellatio talents) Bugsy actually collaborated with quirky Billy Wilkerson. Bugsy had nothing to do with the purchase of the land. Margaret M. Folsom sold a thirty-acre plot off the strip to Wilkerson. Attorney Greg Bautzer brokered the $84,000 deal, and acted as the owner. Wilkerson hired daring Del E. Webb, co-owner of the New York Yankees, to head the Flamingo construction.[16] Surprise partner Bugsy showed up at the construction site a month after the groundbreaking, and brought gifts for Wilkerson.

U.S. Senator Pat McCarran and the movie studios helped supply Webb with the building materials. Items like steel girders and copper tubing were restricted at that time. Neither the Civilian Production Administration nor the Veterans of Foreign Wars could stop this massive undertaking. Many of the hotel builders "suggested" that their suppliers take stock in the new companies, instead of cash.[17]

The design of the Flamingo was derivative of the Beverly Hills Hotel, a main building with a series of thirty-six luxurious private bungalows. Wilkerson initially hired architect Richard Stradelman, and Virginia Hill was the interior decorator. Bugsy wanted the best and Hill wanted to change everything. Tons of marble, tile, and statuary arrived from Italy. The high-end merchandise needed to satisfy the design was extensive; everything Los Angeles had to offer was purchased at a premium. Nothing came cheap, not even the labor, but black market items helped reduce costs. In addition, the plumbing had a million-dollar price tag thanks to private sewer lines for each room. The original heating and air conditioning had to be rebuilt; the housing structure was too small and the system had improper outlets. Funding became an issue as the project escalated. Lansky authorized Harry Rothberg to sell off sixty-six percent of the Flamingo to cover cash flow problems.

Fights ensued between emotionally unstable Wilkerson, Lansky, and Bugsy, who threatened Wilkerson in front of attorney Greg Bautzer: "And before I go, you're gonna go first. And don't take that lightly. I'll kill ya if I don't get that interest."

Fearless Bautzer told Bugsy to pipe down, or else affidavits outlining the meeting would shortly be in the hands of the police, the district attorneys in L.A. and Vegas, the attorney general, the FBI, and that furthermore Bugsy should personally make sure that nothing happened to Wilkerson. Bautzer additionally advised the boys, "And if Mr. Siegel is wise, or his associates here are, they'd better make sure Mr. Wilkerson doesn't accidentally fall down a flight of stairs. They'd better make sure he doesn't sprain an ankle walking off a curb..." Wilkerson received an initial pay off—$300,000.

The Flamingo's final cost was $6,500,000—five million more than the original budget. Vendors had resold stolen deliveries, and the project became a victim of the mob's own vices. Bugsy had to borrow $1,000,000 from an Arizona Bank to pay Del Webb's construction fees.

Wilkerson thought it was absurd to open so soon and on December 26, 1946, the height of the holiday season. The bedrooms weren't ready, and the guests had to stay at the El Rancho or Last Frontier, one more reason to leave the casino early.

The Flamingo Hotel proved a disaster, despite an opening night with toastmaster George Jessel, George Raft, Sonny Tufts, Jimmy Durante, Xavier Cugat's band, and Rosemarie; perhaps too few stars for the celebrity-happy crowd. Bugsy had wanted

Sinatra, who declined, and was exploring opening his own casino. Virginia Hill and Bugsy greeted their guests—who paid fifteen dollars each, including dinner—like royalty; she wore a white crepe formal gown with sparkling gold sequins; he, a tuxedo adorned by a striking white carnation. The high rollers were all in town with stacks of $100 black chips. The tables were hot, the gamblers won early, and they left with their winnings. The casino owners had not yet learned the art of keeping people inside by creating certain moods with sounds and lights. The show budget ran $35,000 each week, with $4,000 extra skimmed from the casino for Cugat. Lansky knew the score by two in the morning; he looked more like a sucker than the people he had hoped to lure to the tables. The hotel lost between $100,000 and $300,000 in its first two weeks. Cugat limped through a five-week run, and the hotel closed. Wilkerson returned to Hollywood.

Things were not looking good for Bugsy.

4.

Bugsy's brash approach alienated many mob figures on both sides of the ethnic divide, and he ferociously fought Lansky over control of the Flamingo.

Author Hank Messick delved into the inside exchanges:

> "Shit on them," said Bugsy. "The Flamingo is my baby. You said so yourself. They'll get their cut, but I don't want them butting in on my territory. Let them go to Reno if they want to." The face of Meyer Lansky went blank, took on a pinched and hungry look. "I didn't hear that," he said in a cold voice. "I hope I never hear it. This is syndicate money you're spending, Ben. Don't forget it." Suddenly aware he had gone too far, Siegel made a visible effort to control himself.

It was too late.

Following the altercation Lansky called Lou "Rody" Rothkopf at the Hollenden Hotel headquarters in Cleveland, and complained about the Bugsy problem.[18] Rothkopf offered this interpretation to Lansky: "It's that bitch. She's driven him out of his mind." Virginia Hill had not curried any favor with the East Coast leaders, and only irritated an already touchy relationship with Bugsy.[19]

"Get word to Mickey," ordered Lansky. "I want a close watch on Ben, night and day." Lansky knew that he could trust Mickey.

When the Flamingo reopened March 27, 1947, everyone already knew about the hit on Bugsy.

Virginia, secretly married to Bugsy, was making travel plans for Paris, a convenient distance from Beverly Hills. Police Chief Clinton H. Anderson cautiously concurred with her knowledge of the hit: "Virginia Hill is alleged to have been familiar with the entire operation ...she was aware that the killing was to happen..." She picked a fight with Bugsy, justifying her flying into the Parisian arms of a champagne dynasty heir.

Bugsy was aware, too. "There's no doubt that Benny felt there was some kind of come-off going to take place," acknowledged Mickey.

Bugsy's independence had clashed with the national crime syndicate. Colleagues like old pal Lansky linked his flawed personality traits to the Big Greenie murder, something that rattled the syndicate. Nobody thought it was worth all the trouble it had caused. Lansky had had talks with him, but he continued to blaze his own reckless path.

Mickey knew it was too late to change Bugsy. "Benny taught me a lot about diplomacy, but he couldn't teach himself."

He was also stealing too much from the wrong people, and that objective fact was crucial to any business decision made by the mob bosses. The hotel was still millions in the red as Bugsy scrambled to raise $1,500,000 in thirty days. He had bounced $150,000 in Bank of Nevada checks made out to Del Webb Construction.

Following a heated meeting with Lansky in Las Vegas, the two agreed to meet again on June 21 in Beverly Hills. Lansky was spotted there the day after the Vegas meet. Bugsy had hopes of maintaining a share in the Flamingo, after turning over the bulk of operations to the mob, or so Lansky would later disclose to insiders.

The day before his demise, Bugsy flew in from Vegas at four in the morning to have Mickey secure more armaments. He wanted to be prepared, and ran down the roster of local muscle who worked for Mickey.

Bugsy spent his last day on earth making the rounds in Beverly Hills. First lieutenant Allen

Smiley chauffeured him to Drucker's for a haircut, to an attorney, and later to the Coldwater Canyon home of pal George Raft, who was raising money for his own motion picture production company. He ended the day at Virginia Hill's sixteen room rented home in Beverly Hills.[20] He treated Smiley and houseguests, twenty-one-year-old Charles "Chick" Hill (Virginia's brother) and girlfriend/secretary Jeri Mason to a trout dinner at Jack's in Ocean Park, a seaside town.

On June 20, 1947, at 10:45 p.m., as forty-two-year-old Bugsy sat in Virginia Hill's home reading the *Los Angeles Times*, a long-range sniper hit him in one of his baby blue eyes with a thirty-caliber high speed carbine bullet (the embellished popular culture description). A proper autopsy revealed that the bullet actually entered the back of his skull, and exited through an eye socket; investigators found the eye across the room. The cause of death was cerebral hemorrhage. It was one of the most gruesome and famous mob murders of the era. According to Florabel Muir, "Four of the nine shots fired that night destroyed a white marble statue of Bacchus on a grand piano, and then lodged in the far wall."

The corner of the newspaper had a tiny advertising sticker that read, "Good night, sleep peacefully, with compliments of Jack's."

The assailant had hid in the shrubbery near a rose trellis and fired nine shots through a fourteen-inch square in the terrace window. Five hit their mark—two in the head. Bugsy remained upright on the flower-patterned, chintz-covered sofa as the blood poured from his face.

Smiley had directed Bugsy to his final seat—the only angle visible from the window. Charles was upstairs with his girlfriend Jeri at the time of the shooting. When they came down, Smiley, sprawled on the floor, yelled, "Douse the lights. They're shooting through the window," and to call the police. A bullet had passed through his coat.

Virginia Hill, identified as an "Alabama Heiress," wouldn't show her face in Beverly Hills after the shooting. Upon her return from abroad, she spent most of her time in Mexico.

Moe Sedway and Gus Greenbaum were inside the Flamingo within one hour of the shooting. Charlie Resnick, Morris Rosen, and Davey Berman also had a future hand in operations. The bosses calmly announced that the hotel was under new ownership.

The day after Bugsy's death, Mickey called Drucker's to make an appointment for a haircut.

Chief Anderson appeared at Mickey's Brentwood home—its value now estimated at $200,000—to ask him who shot Bugsy, although he makes no mention of this in his own book published in 1960, when Mickey was still very much alive and in power.

Mickey appeared visibly shaken and answered the Beverly Hills police chief, "I wish I knew."

To show how upset he was, Mickey drove his fancy Cadillac throughout Los Angeles, and made sure that everyone knew he was looking for Bugsy's killers.[21] Crime mythology bathes in how he pretended to act on news that the killer had decided to hide in the posh Roosevelt Hotel, a place where any action would surely make the papers. The Lilliputian boss pulled a stunt out of the Wild West, and hustled in with his guns brandished, and called the bad guys out. He fired from two forty-five caliber automatic pistols, and made a nouveau design in the ceiling of the already elaborate foyer. Mickey's friends deny that this took place, citing that it was out of character.

Hits were part of the business, and Mickey had to look the other way when the Bugsy plan materialized—likely based on an understanding between Lansky and Dragna.

> People in my line of work always had a reciprocal agreement on certain matters. Like if something had to be looked up or taken care of out here, I was called on by somebody in Chicago or Philadelphia or Boston... If the request went

very far, naturally, it would have to get a real good clearance.

Many people had a lot to gain by eliminating Bugsy. Sedway and Greenbaum were among those who didn't weep over his demise. Weeks before the hit, a worldwide summit meeting took place in Havana, Cuba. Lucky Luciano held court, and discussed the Bugsy problem, which included his skimming on Mexican narcotics points. Theorists suggest that he then privately had called for Bugsy's demise. Some thought that Dragna was in on the hit. Those who knew him better said that it was unlikely that the mediocre career criminal had any direct connection. Lansky tried to pin the rap on Dragna, despite attempting to broker a peace between Dragna and Mickey, who wanted to "hit" his Italian competition. Others claimed that it was Frankie Carbo. Mickey suggested much later that it might have been Frank Costello, who had backed off from business in Los Angeles, opting to let Dragna fight it out with Mickey, who renounced any ties to the Italian operation.

Columnist Sidney Zion was convinced that Lansky had Siegel killed and, of course, that meant that Mickey was in on the hit—he had the most to gain; many thought he had the hit arranged for personal reasons. Newspapers all over the country raised suspicions about him. It was front-page news with scenarios fueled by classic Shakespearean tragedy motivations. Stalwart Fred Sica spoke years later of his conversations with Mickey: "...a little bit longer, maybe, and you might be the boss, eh?"

People all over the country feared that the Bugsy assassination would stir up gang wars in every city, and pressured politicians to act. During interrogatories by the city, state, and federal authorities, Frankie Carbo and others who didn't want to accept Mickey as the new boss blamed him for the Bugsy set-up. H. Leo Stanley, chief investigator of the Los Angeles district attorney's office, was one of the prominent proponents of "Let's blame Mickey." His boss, D. A. William E. Simpson, would have loved to pin anything on Mickey. Simpson's office was convinced that he had Bugsy killed, and based its theory on surveillance conversations recorded in his Brentwood home, particularly remarks made to Alfredo (Fred) Sica.

Stanley hyped what he had for all it was worth:

> In those transcripts, as well as in the tapped phone talks... I understand there are certain references to conversations...arranging release from jail in Fresno...certain individual on $50,000 bail.

Stanley was convinced that the bail money was for the shooter.

Mickey responded to investigator Stanley and others by going public: "I never said anything incriminating." He knew that enough evidence didn't exist. He had copies of all his surveillance tapes—nineteen wax transcriptions—so it was impossible to bluff him. The police eventually backed off, and cited publicly that they did not have the proper evidence to proceed. The FBI corroborated that the local police had nothing on him.

According to Mickey, he had stepped in right away to take over all of Bugsy's operations "on instructions from the people back east." Years later, he waxed emotional for a moment: "Naturally, I missed Benny, but to be honest with you, his getting knocked off was not a bad break for me..."

New boss Mickey had some substantial challenges in Los Angeles. The upcoming battle for control of the Sunset Strip and all it represented would become the bloodiest in the history of Los Angeles. Frank Costello, who liked Mickey, stayed out of it.[22] Once Johnny Rosselli was imprisoned for parole violation charges, only Dragna and Mickey were left to fight for control. Rosselli had made it clear to him that Mickey had to go. Mickey's grandstanding had a sour effect on Rosselli, who confided in a girlfriend, "That Mickey Cohen. He's a disgrace to the underworld."

5.

With Bugsy out of the picture, Mickey received all the public attention. He was the most powerful and visible mob influence on the West Coast. The press enjoyed his antics, and reported on him regularly. Hollywood and its surrounding areas became a city of vice, and he "a gang lord without peer," according to *Life*. He ambitiously wrote editors and journalists, a habit that he would continue the rest of his life; he felt that if anyone printed something about him, he had a duty to let him or her know if the information was "fair and objective." Of course, he would deny that he had anything to do with criminal activity. If a writer questioned his motives or suggested something about his religion, the offending office would find reams of mail from Mickey; some letters were over seventeen pages long. He was as relentless in his journalistic and literary pursuits as he was in his business ventures.

Moe Sedway and Doc Stacher now handled daily operations at the Flamingo, while Mickey took his orders from the national leaders. An FBI report noted that Dragna was leaking information about Mickey's plans to kidnap Sedway, who was in the hospital. He claimed that Mickey was going to hold Sedway for a $100,000 ransom. While nothing materialized, Mickey didn't waste any time taking over the race book at the Flamingo Hotel in Vegas. Even though it was beginning to turn a profit, the casino skimming was too much to handle, and the whole situation looked like a sure loser to insiders. Four months after the grand opening of the hotel, Mickey's cut of the income was $1500 to $2000 a month and his main job was to be certain that the gambling debts were paid.[1]

His success in Los Angeles continued its dependence on a cadre of dishonest politicians who were able to wink and sleep comfortably at the end of the day. Artie Samish, the man who never met a meal he didn't like, helped Mickey every step of the way. He and Mickey backed Fred N. Howser for attorney general in 1947. Howser, who had an impeccable record, had worked for Governor Earl Warren, who saw him as the wrong man for the job because of his mob associations; a Warren-Howser feud persisted for years.[2]

Howser assigned Detective Harry M. Cooper from the Hollywood Bureau to hang around with Mickey and act as a bodyguard, a courtesy of Samish's appeal to Sacramento lobbyists. Mickey did not want any protection from the police; he felt it was more of a liability. With his own coterie of enforcers, the last thing he needed was police interference.

Attorney General Howser had told the police to "lay off Cohen for the time being," according to the FBI. The *New York Times* called the Howser investigation "extensive...pertaining to gangsters and hoodlums, race wire services, the murder of Benjamin (Bugsy) Siegel and other interests of the office pertaining to the Los Angeles vice inquires." The article referred to Mickey as a "key witness in a county grand jury investigation of sustained corruption in the Los Angeles police department." Despite all the publicity, no indictments from the investigation reached Mickey.

The *Nation* reporters were never shy about the realities surrounding Mickey:

> ...everyone is morally implicated in the situation which creates Mickey Cohen and corrupt police departments and does strange things to the press...the general social situation is so corrupt that a modicum of force and bribery...makes it possible for the hoodlums to take over.[3]

Gambling continued to grow, despite the cries by politicians to eliminate it. The State of California, which received revenue from tote machines at the legal tracks, contributed to Mickey's success by assisting in the expansion of wire services, which needed the legal betting operations as much as they did Mickey's bookmaking services. Over 8,000 legal slot machines operated in California alone, and owners paid a $100 federal tax on each device. A sergeant in the Los Angeles Police Department ordered 500,000 punchboards, essentially lottery boards, similar to today's scratch-off versions.

Money and banging heads together didn't satisfy the local gang lord, although he was proud of his success at the latter. Despite his entry into a variety of regular businesses beyond Hollywood's financial trappings, Mickey was dissatisfied with his fronts and had an undying need to be part of the show business milieu that surrounded him. Tinsel Town's pervasive atmosphere proved a more powerful aphrodisiac than politics. Since he was able to maintain a glamorous reputation thanks to those—and there were many—who wanted to embrace gangsters, his access to the inner workings of show business was limitless. Like posh Manhattanite criminal Arnold Rothstein, he wanted to be a patron saint of the arts, thereby solidifying his place in popular culture.[4]

Almost everyone within Hollywood's creative boundaries imagined that he or she could put on a show. Each one, from parking attendants to accountants, had a screenplay in their back pocket. The celebrity-driven environment likewise seduced Mickey, and he made a concerted effort to become a legitimate player in the movie business. He became as interested in promoting a creative property as he was in collecting his Vegas money. Hollywood drove him; it became his ticket to immortality.

His movie and literary interests grew out of his friendship with Ben Hecht, another tinsel town convert.[5] Mickey had already settled in as a celebrity in 1947, when Hecht took him under his Hollywood wing. Hecht had a diverse background, despite having never attended college, which may have accounted for his willingness to embrace someone like Mickey. Their shared interest in Jewish politics would bring them together; Mickey maintained a strong interest in Palestine.

He initially had no idea who Hecht was, but after intermediary Mike Howard, "manager and bodyguard," explained further, and with some convincing by Neddie Herbert, he grew excited. After he and Hecht spoke on the telephone, Mickey agreed to a meeting at Hecht's Oceanside, California, home.

Hecht recalled his first vision of Mickey: "...he had put on weight as an 'underworld king' due to his passion for ice cream and French pastry. He ate little else."

Mickey's demeanor amongst Hollywood elite was nothing like his purported police profiles. Hecht portrayed him as a man at peace: "Outwardly he was a calm, staring man in a dapper pastel suit." Mickey never came on strong in the company of people he respected. He had learned how to carry himself with a quiet dignity within the limitations of his conversational skills and street education.

He was most afraid that Hecht would swindle him and wanted to be sure that he represented only kosher interests in Los Angeles, unlike the "phony Jews" as he called them.

Mickey and Hecht would learn that they were both ghetto children; Hecht had attended Broome Street Number Two public school in one of the worst sections in Manhattan, which is now part of the chic SoHo district.

Hecht observed the gangsters' response after finding out about Broome Street: "A wave of relief seemed to come over them [Howard and Mickey]."

Howard tried to break the ice at the meeting by relating a recent mishap in which Mickey bought a Palestine bronze plaque from a Jewish patriot. The man turned out to be a Chicago con artist, and got away with two hundred of Mickey's cash. Howard then awkwardly presented Mickey's political position to Hecht:

> As soon as Mr. Cohen's friends catch this thief, they will break his head. In the meantime we would like to be of some help to the Jewish situation—if we can be assured we are not goin' to be trimmed. So Mr. Cohen would be obliged if you told him that's what with the Jews who are fighting in Palestine. Mr. Cohen is sorry for the dead Jews in Europe but is not interested in helping them.

Hecht's "outfit" still did not appear legit to them, and they insisted on detailed explanations from him.

Howard further confronted Hecht, one of the highest paid screenwriters in town: "I can't understand why you are having any trouble raising finances in Hollywood for your outfit. The movie studios are run by the richest Jews in the world. They could underwrite this whole Irgun matter overnight." Howard had nailed the political dilemma in Hollywood: local Jews possessed a mixed morality when it came to the Irgun.[6]

Hecht did his best to explain the different strata amongst Jews; many preferred to stay out of international politics. The wealthy Hollywood Jews wanted nothing to do with the fighting, and publicly opposed his American League for a Free Palestine. He explained that he was unable to get a nickel out of Hollywood for the Irgun.

Mickey resented what he called a "highfalutin Jew," and was aware of his effective role as its counterpart. He spoke up: "Knockin' their own proposition, huh?" He decided that he could help, particularly with the backing of the Jewish mob on the national level. He cautiously told Hecht, "I'd like to see you some more. Maybe we can fix up something."

Out of those meetings, Hollywood and the criminal underworld forged another strange bond. Mickey would meet Hecht frequently at his home.

Hecht recalled that he was "diverted, relaxed, even pleased" to have Mickey as a new friend. He described Mickey's life as representing "a certain sanity in a lunacy-whirling world—the sanity of the criminal." Mickey didn't present a hidden agenda, and was a refreshing change to many of the jaded locals.

During the new pals' travails, Hecht introduced Mickey to Otto Preminger, a former actor, and now a well-known producer and director who, Mickey recalled, later needed information for the edgy movie *The Man with the Golden Arm,* which would star Frank Sinatra as a heroin addict.[7]

Mickey and Otto spoke about the horse racing business during a party in Mickey's backyard, a Sunday ritual of Italian food. During his conversation with Otto Mickey received a phone call from Rocky Paladino, and Otto overheard him use the word "laid" in conjunction with "horse." He asked Hecht, "What kind of man is this? What does he mean, he lays horses?" Otto expected the most perverse explanation.

Mickey "humbly" felt that he was an asset to Hecht.

> The writer Ben Hecht was always bringing people to meet me. I guess he thought I was some sort of strength that could help certain people. I don't know how he learned about me or anything, but I guess there was always a lot about me in the papers.

Mickey and Hecht would take long night drives along the coast with Neddie, and sometimes stopped at an all-night ice cream stand Mickey owned. Hecht was sensitive to his complicated and privately sullen friend, and knew that Mickey's life offered little diversion from his conflicted and stressful activities.

During the period of Mickey's initial friendship with Hecht, the FBI listed his illicit income sources as gambling, shakedowns, proceeds from robberies, payments for strong-arm jobs, and prostitution, something he always denied. His gambling interests included an elaborate betting pyramid centered on the racetracks. Prostitution was something the boys from back east continued to expect when in town, and a cornerstone of Las Vegas.

It grew in Los Angeles, ranging from the low-end burlesque houses and bars, catering to intoxicated servicemen and husbands eager to arrange an assignation at one of the local hotels, to fancy call girl services. Many semi-pros were employed by movie studios as bit players, but had larger assignments that included socializing with visiting exhibitors, executives, and local politicians. The party girls could also find extra income by frequenting bars where the bartender could arrange dates by phone. All this took place while most of the country was gearing up for one of its most provincial decades. The freewheeling attitude toward sex in Los Angeles was practically unheard of in other major cities. The homosexual population grew, and would find a comfortable nightlife at places like the Maxwell Café and the local Flamingo. Authors Jack Lait and Lee Mortimer would blame "the impressionable youth of both sexes, which reflects the manners and mores of the movie colony…quick to take up filth as a fad." The naïve authors remarked how husky cowpunchers, rugged U.S.C.

football stars, middle-class homeowners, voters, Negroes, Mexicans, Chinese, Japanese, important politicians, leading industrialists, and too many movie personnel could all be taken in by the increase in local perversion, including the questionable sexuality of the new "great wave of fairies and lesbians."

Misogynist Mickey regularly set up famous actresses, including Marilyn Monroe and Lana Turner, with many of the young men who worked for him. He filmed them having sex, so that he could sell the movies on the black market. If he wanted to influence an actress's activities, he would threaten to make the film public. He was involved in regular shakedowns of local prostitutes; he "borrowed" almost $10,000 from a relative of one girl. Other times he played the role of benefactor, more consistent with his projected public image. The local environment and the social permissiveness of Los Angeles enhanced his lascivious activities.

Mickey socialized with many women, countless of whom thought that his show business connections could help them. One nefarious girlfriend was Elizabeth (Beth) Short, the "Black Dahlia," who fancied black outfits with fire red lipstick and nail polish. A calculating sexual tease with show business aspirations, she finagled her way into the lives of well-known movie and mob people who paid her way. Many, like movie star Franchot Tone, struck out when it came to sex with her. Speculation on her sex life ranges from prostitute to seductive virgin, the latter based on autopsy reports. Mickey and Short liked to hang out at the Spanish Kitchen on Beverly Boulevard. Popular Short became a brutal murder victim in 1947; her body, severed in half, had the appearance of a well-planned scalpel murder. The notorious and ghastly murder remains unsolved.

Routine rousts took place, like the one on November 15. Mickey gave his word that Jimmy Fratianno, Nick Satullo, James Regace, Harry Brook, Samuel Bontempe, and Sidney Dine would all leave town. Fratianno had already served eight years for robbery in Ohio, and Satullo had served six years for murder. Regace gave his occupation as a haberdasher. The police claimed that this was the beginning of a national push against criminals.

Mickey's most famous legit business was his elegant men's clothing store on Santa Monica Boulevard, Michael's Exclusive Haberdashery, which opened in 1947. Reporters liked to chide him by writing that all the suits in the store were his size. Since the mugs needed a hangout, the haberdashery was open twenty-four hours a day. The FBI and Los Angeles police all knew that it was Mickey's headquarters, but nobody under his tutelage was ever seriously pinched, indicted, or prosecuted for any activities stemming from inside the haberdashery, despite the FBI's 1947 claim that he was personally responsible for no less than seven murders. His other businesses now included a jewelry store and several supermarkets. The FBI confessed that he was the quintessential entrepreneur of his generation; he had his hand in anything that made money.

Many investigators, including the California Crime Commission, and several reporters who fought against Mickey's takeover, paid no attention to the developing mobster hierarchy and its rapidly changing structure. While he continually moved up, some refused to accept the obvious: he had made it to boss. Former Brooklyn prosecutor Turkus, who was not alone in his thinking, despised Mickey's manipulation of the media and his success:

> ...the small shot who goes for the sandwiches when the big boys have their hotel-room sessions... His efforts appear to have been about as weighty as Mickey Mouse... It is just that Mickey revels in getting his name in the papers; Dragna hides from a headline... There have been some recent news-wire stories, attendant on attempts on his life, which sought to picture the undersized loudmouth as Bugsy's heir... Mickey

Cohen thought he was just the man to fill Bugsy's shoes... The real power, though, appears to be Dragna—and no one knows it better than Mickey."

The last part of the evaluation was true, and Mickey clearly had ideas about how to resolve the future in his favor. He was determined to prove wrong anyone who had completely misjudged the balance of power after Bugsy's demise. His methods were way ahead of his time, and he had developed unique communication skills that few public figures possessed.

Despite his own self-doubts, he had become an international celebrity. His activities provided a steady stream of headlines. "The fastidious little gambler had captured the imaginations of people all over the world," wrote journalist pal Muir. People who read about him wanted to protect him, and lived in denial when it came to his detractors. Muir confessed that he fascinated her and she took full advantage of his insatiable need for publicity, which didn't hurt her regular readership, while she enjoyed countless nights out on the town with her subject.

He wasn't quite inside the Varsity, Clan, or, later, Rat Pack. He could not garner the public's worship that was reserved for the most celebrated entertainers. Despite his less-than-handsome physical appearance, he did cut a dashing figure in extraordinarily tailored suits, which helped him assimilate further into the entertainment crowd. He continued to lead the fantasy life that the public suspected of entertainers. He shopped in the right places, tended to his hair and nails at the fancy establishments, and mingled with celebrities. He also became a fan of some entertainers, and influenced their careers.

Mickey's criminal instincts would always keep him in his own special category of celebrity, and in trouble. Ironically, by breaking the law, he received the fame he desired from those whom the laws protected. Despite his tiny number of convictions, the local police regularly rousted him without due process and the FBI tracked his every move. Considering his control over illicit businesses that had expanded well outside the provincial boundaries of Los Angeles, it was remarkable that he continued to survive without prosecution and permanent incarceration.

6.

Mickey's relationship with Ben Hecht led to his continual involvement with Jewish causes. Beginning in 1941, Hecht had developed firm relations with the Irgun, an Israeli defense organization. Peter Bergson, Samuel Merlin, and Yitzhak Ben-Ami had asked him to help in their project to create a Jewish army in Palestine and to make American Jews aware of the Holocaust.[1]

Mickey became directly involved with Menachem Begin and the Irgun. The future of Palestine (Israel) became an obsession for him:

> Now I got so engrossed...that I actually pushed aside a lot of my activities and done nothing but what was involved with this Irgun wars... There were dinners held in Boston, Philadelphia, Miami. And plenty of armament and equipment was collected that you could possibly get.

The neophyte Zionist wanted to influence Jewish politics at the international level, and like everything else he attempted, he was fearless when it came to Palestinian politics. Despite his business success, his personal net worth had more to do with being a Jew than the balance in his bank account. Because of his torturous mixed morality, he remained Jewish first and mobster second, and Jewish leaders, including rabbis, knew they could count on him for help.

The Jewish mob and their business associates were an enormous help in solidifying the future of the soon-to-be Israeli state. None of the underworld activities involving Israel could have taken place without the help of ex-haberdasher President Harry Truman. Mickey had open run on the docks, and was able to get supplies, even government surplus, ready for shipping. The East Coast was in full swing via Albert Anastasia and Charlie "The Jew" Janowsky. Meyer Lansky orchestrated a significant amount of gun hustling from New York. In New Jersey, Harold "Kayo" Konigsberg was on call for the Irgun.

Writer Sidney Zion lamented the overall lack of cooperation in the United States: "...that scores of Jewish outlaws were busy running guns around Mr. Truman's blockade while their liveried Jewish cousins shook their heads in shame or sat in those Frank Lloyd Wright temples rooting for the English." History showed that "the American Jewish leaders raised hardly a peep while their brothers were melted to soap." American Jews at the time were preoccupied with their daily lives, and hardly paid attention to the initially sparse reports of horror coming out of Europe, downplayed by the American media. Assimilation proved more important than separation, while many, concerned for their own security, did not want to become the focus of growing anti-Semitism in the U.S.

Irgun leaders asked Mickey for advice, and he made suggestions on how to handle the politics with the British, whose position remained cold: they didn't care how many Jews died, so long as the Arab oil survived, and the Jews stayed out of Palestine. He suggested hanging British officers in a public area during the worst part of the conflict. The gruesome advice was nonetheless effective and contributed to the British ultimately leaving Palestine.

In June 1947, just prior to Bugsy's murder, Mickey headed up a fundraising drive for the Irgun. "Through my connections I made everybody throughout the country—the Italians, the Jews, the Irish—set up whatever positions there were to be helpful to the Israel cause."

The top mobster brass attended a gala, and didn't quibble. Mickey was powerful enough to throw a benefit with a significant turnout. Slapsy Maxie's

Café, the famous off-Sunset Strip club run by Mickey, hosted the lavish affair. The front man/manager, Max Gould, lent the club free of charge for the event. Borscht belt entertainer Lou Holtz was the master of ceremonies for the criminal and show business royalty.

Jimmy "The Weasel" Fratianno recalled the unique dinner:

> ...The place's packed. I've never seen so many Jewish bookmakers in one place in my life. Abe Benjamin's there, Morey Orloff, Ben Blue, Martha Raye, Danny Thomas. Sitting at our table's the chief of police of Burbank and his wife, Mickey and LaVonne. Neddie Herbert and his wife, and me and Jewel. And I'm sitting next to Mickey.

A weakened Ben Hecht (he had a recent hospital stay to remove his gall bladder) "addressed a thousand bookies, ex-prize fighters, gamblers, jockeys, touts, and all sort of lawless and semi-lawless characters; and their womenfolk" for forty-five minutes.

After a few more speeches and remarks by Mickey's own rabbi, Menachem Begin—on the lam for the King David Hotel bombing in Israel—stood before the throngs of criminals to add authenticity to the cause.[2]

Mickey had plugged into a fundraising system that had existed for generations. The tradition goes back as far as biblical Isaac, who was the first man to give up one tenth of his earnings for charity. When the pitchmen had exhausted the introductions, Holtz looked to Mickey to make the first pledge, a tried and true method of fundraising to solicit higher or matching pledges.[3]

The methodology arranged by Mickey and his partners had its own demanding twist. Cohort Howard had told Hecht that the fix was in: "Each and everybody here has been told exactly how much to give to the cause of the Jewish heroes. And you can rest assured there'll be no welshers."

Mickey started the ball rolling at $25,000, a substantial amount. "Angels" Bugsy and Samish quickly pledged $10,000 each.

Fratianno recalled the chaos:

> After that, forget about it. Everybody's pledging thousands. Even the bookmakers are pledging five and ten grand. They know Mickey's running the show and they're going to have to pay. I see all this shit going on and I ain't going to pledge nothing. So Mickey kicks me and says "Pledge fifteen thousand."

Fratianno answered, "You're fucking nuts."

Mickey made it clear that he would cover the money.

The apprentice fundraiser gave Hecht a shot in the arm and told him to "Make another speech and hit 'em again."

Hecht declined, citing his recuperation.

Mickey next pushed Howard towards the stage and told him to make an announcement. "Tell 'em they're a lot o' cheap crumbs and they gotta give double."

The estimated amount raised at a series of benefits taking place during that brief period reached well over $1,000,000. The single fundraiser estimates covered a wide range, from $200,000 to $800,000. Many raised eyebrows focused on the take—as much for the huge sums as for who had orchestrated the on-demand drive. Finger pointing and false accounting accusations ran the gamut from total swindle to authentic generosity.

Despite all the good will, Fratianno came away claiming the whole thing was a fraud. Perhaps it does take a thief to catch one, but he was no pal of Mickey's, and never hesitated in later years to diminish him. They worked and occasionally hung out together, but he wouldn't have minded if Mickey suddenly vanished or ended up in a coffin. Fratianno, a product of Cleveland's Little Italy, could not relate to the Jewish mob, many of whom grew up in places like Brownsville or the Lower East Side of Manhattan, nor what it was like to be a Jew and to have just lived through the Holocaust.

He confronted Mickey directly.

> The next day I see Mickey and I says, "What's the scam all about?" He says, "Jimmy, this ain't no scam. This money's for the Jews." I says, "Mickey, don't give me this horseshit. There's no way you're going to let eight hundred grand slip through your fingers. Not in a million fucking years." But he swears it's on the level and now I'm wondering how this guy's going to pull it off.

Months after the fundraiser, Fratianno, who said that Mickey was sitting on a million dollars, claimed that a story appeared in the *Herald* that delineated how the boat carrying the supplies for the Jews had sunk. This added fuel to Fratianno's claim. His paranoia ran so deep that he suggested that Mickey had a plant at the newspaper, someone he saw socially, and she would print whatever he wanted. He believed that the reported sinking of the supply ship for Israel was all part of a grand plan, beginning with the fundraiser.

Fratianno outlined the scenario for author Ovid Demaris:

I think to myself, "You cocksucker, I know your game." The way I see it, Mickey made up a story about buying guns and ammunition for the Jews with the million raised at the benefits and then said the boat sank. A few unknown people died, some were saved, and it gets printed in the press. I says, "Mickey, congratulations. You've just pulled off the biggest, cleanest fucking score I've ever seen made." And he looks at me, just squinting, you know, and for a split second there's this big shit-eating grin on his face. But he says, "Jimmy, you've got me all wrong. The story's right here in the paper." I says, "Mickey, with your bullshit you better hold on to that paper, it might come in handy when you've got to wipe your mouth."

Yitzhak Ben-Ami, who headed the Irgun's European-based illegal immigration operations, took issue with Fratianno. In 1947, the Irgun sent Ben-Ami to the United States to assist the American League for a Free Palestine, the Irgun's funding and propaganda arm in the United States. According to him, Fratianno did not know the amount of money raised or the national distributions.

Herb Brin, former investigative reporter for the *Los Angeles Times*, disagreed emphatically with Fratianno's critical appraisal of Mickey's sincerity.

"I knew how he [Mickey] was and what he was. But when we talked about Israel, he was a different person. He had tears in his eyes once when we talked about Israel."

Journalist Al Aronowitz felt that his relationship with Mickey had as much to do with their own religious backgrounds as anything else:

> Oh, I know he killed people and he was a Yiddish *momser* [bastard] and he was just plain no good. But I was a kid writer who loved colorful characters... I also related on the level of our Jewishness in the same way African-Americans call one another "Bro." Mickey and I both grew up in immigrant Orthodox Jewish households and, in my heart of hearts, I was rooting for Mickey as a Jew who had achieved gangster stardom in an Italian underworld.

The facts surrounding the ship story also do not support Fratianno's critical claims. A ship later chosen for the delivery of supplies was the *Altalena*,[4] the pen name of writer Vladimir Zeev Jabotinsky,[5] who had helped create the Jewish fighting brigades in both World Wars, and the Irgun Zvai Leumi militia.[6]

Modern Hecht biographer William MacAdams and others accepted Fratianno's critical description, and treated the matter as if two ships existed—Mickey's mystery ship and the *Altalena*. Despite all the contrary information, Fratianno remained hell bent on characterizing Mickey as a thief[7] and a liar, and the Jewish fundraising effort as a fraud.[8] That didn't stop him from attending Mickey's weekly bagel-and-cream-cheese brunches.

However, Mickey's fundraising methods would cost him his standing in the eyes of influential Jews. Many respectable leaders were uncomfortable with his addition to the international political mix. Jewish circles tried to drum him out of his political relationships. His character was too extreme for scores of upper-crust Jews, many of whom were against the Irgun anyway, and others simply wanted nothing to do with him because of his criminal background.

Mickey's response to his diminished Jewish social standing was logical and businesslike. The unhappy Jewish groups contacted attorneys Sam Rummel and partner Vernon Ferguson, and asked if they could intercede and convince Mickey to curtail his activities.[9] The Jewish leadership made it clear that they would see to it that he would go to jail, but he paid little attention to the threats, which ultimately amounted to nothing.

Most people in the Jewish-cause trenches did not have a problem doing business with Mickey. Yehuda

Arazi was the arms buyer for the Haganah, and made the realistic position of his organization crystal clear: "In my business we can't be too fussy who we do business with. Sometimes they're not nice people."

Mickey's activities were not limited to fundraising, and he later recalled some of the details: "Through my connections, I was able to send armaments to Israel. There were a couple of Irish kids, expert in dynamite. They went over as a favor to me and taught those young Israel soldiers how to use the stuff. And I sent over three pilots."

Due in part to their efforts, many Jewish gangsters lived to see the creation of Israel and its survival as a strong Jewish State; it was a rewarding victory for the Jewish mob. Years later, Mickey would proudly display a silver cigarette box engraved with, IN GRATITUDE, TO A FELLOW FIGHTER FOR HEBREW FREEDOM "MICKEY COHEN," FROM THE HEBREW COMMITTEE OF NATIONAL LIBERATION, awarded June 1, 1958.

7.

Mickey's long-standing relationship with Sinatra, ultimately the Rat Pack, and their entourage, highlighted the perverse intermingling of entertainers and mobsters that took place every night in his clubs. Sinatra's manager George Evans was forever trying to squelch stories linking Frank to Mickey. When detectives found Sinatra's phone number in his address book Mickey answered simply, "Why, he's a friend of mine."

While Sinatra had always been cool to Bugsy, he remained close with Mickey and respected his power and social opinions. Sinatra had immense popularity, charm, charisma, and a questionable high-class reputation—all things Mickey desired. He was a new breed of Hollywood mobster, as vibrant and flamboyant as any entertainer. Each one wanted a piece of the other.

During the period of Mickey's fundraising efforts, Sinatra[10] asked him for help with his social life, in particular his soured relationship with Ava Gardner. The two industry powerhouses met at night in Mickey's luxurious Brentwood home. He knew that his house was under surveillance, but it did not deter either one of them, and a one-on-one personal talk ensued.

Sinatra appealed to his unlikely dating advisor to intervene. "Lookit. I want you to do me this favor. I want you to tell your guy Johnny Stompanato to stop seeing Ava Gardner."

Sinatra didn't know that he had little to worry about when it came to Stompanato, who made the Hollywood rounds, dating many aspiring and already famous actresses. He was aware that Mickey could control Stompanato.

Mickey responded cordially, "I treated him like a friend." He told Sinatra that he didn't like to mix into anything having to do with broads, and advised Sinatra to return to his family.

Mickey saw himself as an advisor for the lovelorn. "I actually felt at all times that Frank was going to go back to Nancy where he really belongs. I love Frank and I have a very great respect for him, and even when he was at his worst, I was his best friend... I mean, that is what a friend would say. Besides, I had troubles of my own."

Sinatra chose booze, mostly at Ciro's, to soothe his eventual loss of Ava Gardner, the only breakup that showed his sentimental side.

Mickey's relationship with Sinatra solidified further when times became difficult for the singer in the late forties and early fifties, a period that included serious vocal problems and a decline in popularity.

He provided a resurrection testimonial dinner at the Beverly Hills Hotel; he had the clout to bring out the big names. Because he liked Sinatra, Mickey spent a great deal of time and effort organizing the dinner and made sure the place was packed. It was an impressive tribute.

Mickey later reflected on the troubled times for the crooner: "When Frank was going pretty bad, when he was kind of discouraged...I brought in his father and mother, and they put their arms around me and kissed me the same as they did Frank. His voice was even faltering a bit at the time... I was close to tears myself because his voice was really bad... A lot of people who were invited to that Sinatra testimonial, that should have attended, but didn't, would bust their nuts in this day to attend a Sinatra testimonial. A lot of them would now kiss Frank's ass... I really felt that he just had to find himself again."

Mickey's club operations included the Rhum Boogie on Highland Avenue—the club's name likely copied from the Chicago version associated with boxer Joe Louis. Run by Mike Howard, the club featured popular black acts. Mickey was proud of the fact that John Barrymore was a frequent customer. Barrymore liked to pick up washerwomen who were working the night shift in nearby office buildings and take them all out to dinner.

Mickey's Slapsy Maxie's was located near cross street La Brea in the Miracle Mile district on Wilshire Boulevard. Boxer-turned-actor namesake "Slapsy" Maxie Rosenbloom, nicknamed by Damon Runyon, was the source material for the Big Julie character in *Guys and Dolls*. Now the Beverly Cinema, the 4,000-square-foot Slapsy Maxie club helped launch the careers of Jackie Gleason, Phil Silvers, Danny Thomas and Joe E. Lewis, the latter famous for having his throat slashed by the mob over a contract dispute, and ultimately receiving a testimonial dinner by the Friars in 1950. Lewis was famous for his lines, "Behind every successful man is a surprised mother-in-law... Behind every great woman is a great behind."

The other fronts for the Slapsy Maxie club were clothiers Charlie and Sy Devore, who dressed the soon-to-be Rat Pack in sharkskin suits, and provided the wardrobe for many future television shows. Mickey claimed to have only lent the Devores some cash to get started, perhaps twenty-five thousand dollars. Despite his denials, the cocky impresario maintained a certain number of investment points in Slapsy's and other clubs, as in any structured investment. That number was always subject to change, particularly if the headliners increased nightly revenues.

Mickey helped launch the careers of several popular entertainers. The Devores liked the Martin and Lewis act enough to ask him to finance the venture. Dean Martin and former Brownsville resident Jerry Lewis made their first appearance on the West Coast on August 9, 1948, at Slapsy Maxie's, after a huge splash at the Copa in New York. Before the Copa, Martin and Lewis had appeared at the Five O'Clock Club in Atlantic City, owned by Skinny D'Amato,[11] who never charged admission to celebrities. They had played all the mob-run joints: the Riviera in North Jersey, and the Chez Paree in Chicago.

Mickey also helped by filling the club tables with his on-demand entourage. The audience, which needed little coaxing to see the most remarkable act in show business history, included Barbara Stanwyck, Humphrey Bogart, Lauren Bacall, Jane Wyman, Ronald Reagan, James Cagney, Clark Gable, Donald O'Connor, Debbie Reynolds, Gene Kelly, Fred Astaire, Rita Hayworth, Orson Welles, Harpo and Chico Marx, Edward G. Robinson, Bob Hope, Bing Crosby, Carmen Miranda, Al Jolson, Mel Tormé, Count Basie, Judy Garland, Mickey Rooney,

Spencer Tracy, Greer Garson, William Powell, Billy Wilder, June Allyson, and Gloria DeHaven. At a pool party at George Raft's house earlier that same day Martin and Lewis had met Loretta Young, Edward G. Robinson, Veronica Lake, Mona Freeman, William Holden, William Demarest, and Dorothy Lamour.

Guy and Angela Crocetti, Dean's parents, were ringside.

The magical act debuted with the energetic Dick Stabile orchestra, a perfect match for the zany Martin and Lewis. Slapsy Maxie bartender Dick Martin was inspired to copy Dean's act; the timing and character he created would carry him to *Laugh-In* fame with partner Dan Rowan.

Joan Crawford was also in the audience the night Martin and Lewis brought down the house at Slapsy Maxie's, and remarked, "That Dean Martin is rather attractive," but she made it clear to her journalist friend Larry Quirk that wild and screwball Jerry Lewis would probably make a better lover.

Sinatra's first take on Martin and Lewis was not entirely enthusiastic: "The dago's lousy, but the little Jew is great."[12]

Martin[13] and Lewis[14] negotiated a movie deal with producer Hal Wallis, a record contract with Capitol, and a television show with NBC. Mickey used his power in the entertainment business to help the funny duo join the professional unions. It was easy for Mickey to ask for favors; he controlled goon squads working at a number of unions, including A.F. of L., which paid big protection money.[15] At first comedian Lou Costello balked, and complained about an unpaid debt from Martin. Mickey maintained a close enough relationship with Costello, who also maintained ties to New Jersey mobster Willie Moretti, to have him step aside and not hinder the careers of Martin and Lewis, who gave a command performance at Moretti's daughter's wedding in New Jersey.

Despite all the occasional grandstanding by the authorities regarding Mickey's hard times, he and his troublemakers were doing well. A new, more luxurious haberdashery was in the works at the 8800 block of Sunset Boulevard, and Mickey couldn't wait to permanently move to the hot Sunset Strip address near Ciro's and Mocambo.

The topping on this eclectic period was another hit—August 18, 1948. This time it was more public, at Mickey's haberdashery. The folklore surrounding this hit typified the multiple versions of mob events reported by newspapers, authors, eyewitnesses, and Mickey himself. Cursory details of the Fratianno version sound surprisingly realistic, since it involved one of the many benefits of mobster life: a never-ending ticket source for sporting events and shows. *Annie Get Your Gun* at the Greek Theater was the hot ticket that year. Mickey had seen the show and was recommending it to his associates. Fratianno brought his wife and daughter with him when he visited Mickey's shop to pick up tickets for the show. Fratianno, recently released from the Ohio State Penitentiary, suffered from tuberculosis, and Mickey had paid his hospital bills at a sanitarium in the San Fernando Valley.

Mickey boasted to Fratianno, "Be my guests. They don't cost me nothin' anyway. I can get all the free tickets I want. Best seats in the house, too. I got you third row, center aisle."

Fratianno's version of the shooting contradicts what the police and crime researchers had surmised. While the innocent ticket exchange took place, a hit squad was waiting outside. If this story was true, Fratianno exercised poor judgment when he shook hands with Mickey, who quickly headed off to the washroom to disinfect, a scenario that somewhat corroborates several creative memories of the incident.

Frank DeSimone waited outside for the signal from Fratianno. Once Fratianno's family was out of range and well down the boulevard, Frank "The Bomp" Bompensiero joined DeSimone outside the shop. The Bomp resembled a B-movie version of a Los Angeles hit man: he wore a white Panama hat and sunglasses and he had a reputation as one of the most feared hit men in the country, which made him a popular choice to kill mobsters. Fratianno said that The Bomp "had buried more bones than could be found in the brontosaurus room of the Museum of Natural History."

From the sales floor of the haberdashery Hooky Rothman spotted the gunmen and rushed outside to confront the two plug-uglies. When they tried to push past Rothman, he took a swing at The Bomp's sawed-off shotgun; The Bomp fired and blew off part of Hooky's face. Hooky was shot a second time as he struggled to his feet.

The *Los Angeles Times* stated simply that Hooky "was blasted fatally with a shotgun by gunmen as he *opened the door* of Cohen's newest shop at 8800 Sunset Blvd" and referred to the larger haberdashery location as "in the luxurious office of Michael (Mickey) Cohen's...heart of The Strip." The entrance to Mickey's office was actually around the corner on side street Palm Avenue, below the street level of the Sunset Boulevard haberdashery. (Italics added.)

Police officers found Hooky in a pool of blood; his bloody handprints marked the wall above him, and another trail of blood lined the stairs to Mickey's office. Revisionists love to create the image of him felled amongst the fine silken menswear. Doctors at

West Hollywood Emergency Hospital pronounced thirty-six-year-old Hooky dead.

During the fracas, two of Mickey's thugs, Al "Slick" Snyder and Jimmy Rist, initially reported to have been watching television, were also injured. Rist was a jack-of-all-trades member of the group. Snyder's role was always a mystery, although every gang tolerated soldiers, hangers-on, or gofers who remained faithful to the cause.

Mickey had originally told journalist Florabel Muir that *he* had been making a long distance telephone call when the hit began. He had handed the telephone to Snyder, and instructed him to wait until the party on the other line answered, while he went to the washroom. When he heard what sounded like shotgun or machine-gun fire, he stepped from the washroom and saw a man running out the front of the building. Hooky was already wounded, slumped on the sidewalk, and Snyder hid under a desk, where he was shot.

Mickey's later revisionist version was no Annie-get-your-gun: "Hooky got killed one night when I had been home late for dinner. I pulled up to the temporary haberdashery, and I looked through the big window where Slick Snyder was sitting at the desk. As I got out of the car, Slick is on the phone and I can see he's telling the operator, 'He just pulled up,' or something like that. Hooky took the car and I jumped into the store." He corroborated that Hooky had tried to grab the shotgun, but contradicted himself further by telling Muir that he had slammed the washroom door shut after the first shots, and laid down on the floor with his feet braced so the door couldn't open. He summarized: "They shot Slick first because when he was at the phone, they thought he was me..." He also later claimed that he saw Rist tackle the gunman who fired on Snyder. "Then I heard another blast outside. It was Jimmy Rist that got hit. They thought they hit him in the head, but they just shot off a piece of his ear."

Sheriff's deputies arrested Mickey, Rist, Snyder, Sol Davis, a "store clerk" who returned from a drive-in diner across the street, and Meyer Horowitz, manager of the haberdashery, for suspicion of murder. Walker Hannon of the Sheriff's Department first took Mickey's statement. The police later tracked down Mike Howard, who allegedly also acted as a store manager and buyer for the haberdashery. Authorities soon released the boys from County Jail.

Chief of Sheriff's Detectives Norris Stensland dragged Mickey to a local West Hollywood substation for a quick interview. Mickey's version on the whereabouts of Hooky before the hit differed from Rist's.

He initially told the detectives, "They were out to get me."

When police grilled Slick Snyder inside General Hospital, he refused to tell them anything, except that he was a haberdasher. Mickey tried in vain to have Snyder moved. Doctors said that his shoulder and right arm would not tolerate the trauma, stating that they hadn't eliminated the possibility of amputating his arm. His doctors requested that the police at least release him from the prison ward.

Mickey told reporters at the hospital, "I have no idea why anybody would want to bump Hooky or me off."

Reporters hypothesized that Mickey's poachers had held up too many competitor bookies, and compared the shooting to Bugsy's demise, which remained unsolved.

The talk of the town became, *Why didn't they get to Mickey?* Many authors accepted the simple answer: he had hid in one of the lavatory stalls. The convenient take was somewhat unrealistic, because trained hit men weren't shy when it came to aiming a few blasts at john doors or breaking them down.

Mickey explained why the shooters left without being sure that they got him: Rist was able to get control of a pistol, and the shooters were amateurs. He told Muir, "If they had been real operators and not such cowardly rats they could have walked up the alley and stuck their guns in through the window and blasted us all. I got a good look at the face of the man who came in first, and as long as I live I will never forget it." Most reports say that the room was dim, making a hit from the outside difficult.

Ballistics experts Sergeant James Layne and Lieutenant Fred Wolfe studied the thirty-eight caliber slugs, and concluded that the bullets matched those of the assailant's gun supplied by Rist.

Groman's Mortuary, 830 W. Washington Boulevard, housed Hooky's body. His brother Louis planned for services the next day, as soon as relatives could arrive from the East Coast.

Mickey detractors claim that he had Hooky set up, and their friendship was questionable, more Shakespearean tragedy than a Norman Rockwell painting. The California Crime Study Commission was also convinced that he had it in for his pal. The Commission claimed that he had ordered Hooky beaten in the past and concluded that the bookie boss had set up the hit. Mickey's friends said that it was unlikely that he would harm Hooky. Fratianno and Dragna, the notable people behind the attack, were not fond of Mickey, and the hit likely had nothing to do with Hooky.

Hooky's surviving brothers did not hold a grudge. At the funeral his brother Babe nodded to Mickey and murmured, "You don't have to say anything. Hooky died the way he wanted. He lived for you, and he died for you the way he wanted."

The experience shocked Mickey, who had been in high spirits pending the completion of his new haberdashery.

He became a hot news item. The FBI commented on the headline attention: "He received sensational publicity in August, 1948, following the assassination of his bodyguard Harry (Hooky) Rothman, supposedly by rival gangsters, and the wounding of two other associates at Cohen's place of business on Sunset Boulevard, Los Angeles."

Police seized Mickey's "bluebook," essentially a list of contacts. Lieutenant Garner Brown of the sheriff's homicide detail began a tedious process of calling and questioning everyone whose name appeared in the book. The list also contained all of Mickey's celebrity contacts, the unlisted telephone numbers of politicians, prizefighters, newspapermen, and Hollywood stars, creating an awkward set of circumstances for the investigators. Chief Detective Norris Stensland reassured the public that no wholesale arrests of names listed in the bluebook would take place, which reduced rumors that had appeared in the papers and alarmed Mickey's celebrity circle.

The local police arrested Mickey three separate times in conjunction with the hit on Hooky, suspicion of murder, suspicion of conspiracy to commit murder, and conspiracy to obstruct justice; assault with a deadly weapon; and robbery. Even with the piling on of charges, nothing harmful to him materialized; his legal team proved successful again. The FBI also begged off the situation.

Mickey established extra security precautions at the haberdashery. He installed bulletproof doors, steel walls, and an elaborate burglar alarm. He stationed an around-the-clock guard on the premises. A steel-plated door separated the sales floor from his office, which was finished with walnut paneling, a ceiling-suspended television, and indirect lighting. He usually sat at a circular desk in an oversized swivel chair, under a picture of President Franklin D. Roosevelt.

In a new roust on September 2, 1948, police arrested Mickey's friend, actor Robert Mitchum, who was charged with possession of marijuana while in the company of two sexy employees of madam Brenda Allen[16]: twenty-five-year-old dancer Vicki Evans and twenty-year-old actress Lila Leeds.[17] Real estate agent Robin Ford was also at the West Hollywood Hills Ridpath Drive bash.

Mitchum told reporters that his career was "all washed up."

Mitchum biographer Lee Server discussed the famous case in unflattering terms for Mickey: "...was widely understood that Mickey Cohen, king of the dope, prostitution, and gambling rackets, had a sizable percentage of LA city and county law enforcement in his pockets..." Mitchum never outright accused Mickey of a setup, but Server was clear: "a connect-the-dots conspiracy theory; that the events leading up to Ridpath Drive were engineered by a vengeful ex-associate, mobster Mickey Cohen, and some corrupt faction in the Sheriff's department ready to do Mickey's bidding."

The D.A. was convinced that madam Brenda Allen, herself a shapely redhead, was helping Mickey use the call girls for blackmail by recording and photographing the sex action with unknowing johns. He had several young men in his employ who helped set up these salacious sessions and sexual blackmail provided a steady stream of cash from distraught husbands, caught in the act with Allen's bevy of young beauties.

Mickey's boys were frequently in and out of trouble. On November 1, 1948, Lieutenant William Burns' special gangster unit jailed Mickey and five pals. Officers picked up the gang at the haberdashery and whisked them off to the Central

Jail on violation of Section 137 of the Penal code, which "prohibits influencing of witnesses' testimony by threat, violence, or bribery." The arresting officers threw in a narcotics charge for Max Rothman. Others arrested were James Regace, Sol Davis, and Davey Ogul. Police later grabbed thirty-five-year-old Jimmy Rist at Mickey's Café Continentale on Santa Monica Boulevard.

The officers nearly fell to the floor when the guests surrendered their pocket cash. Mickey removed slightly over three thousand dollars from his custom-tailored trousers. Max Rothman had forty-one hundred and change, while impoverished Regace barely counted to three hundred and fifty, Ogul nearly one hundred, Rist a few cents shy of sixty bucks, and pauper Sol Davis had only ten dollars and fifteen cents.

The new arrests related to gambler William Petroff's beating on August 30. Police suspected that Joe Sica and Robert Iannone had roughed up the card player. Nothing transpired because the victim later told police Lieutenant Burns that it was all a big mistake and that the beating was part of a drunken brawl.

Then Petroff flipped, and told Chief Deputy D.A. S. Ernest Roll that Mickey and his goons had threatened him. He told the authorities how he had earlier met with Mickey, Regace, Rist, Davis, and one of Mickey's attorneys at a ranch home near Malibu.

In order to insure Petroff's cooperation Mickey tried to pay him off, saying, "Don't you know I can have you killed in five minutes? You'd better keep in line. Don't you want to stay alive around this town?" Mickey gave Petroff fifty dollars and emphasized that he was to repeat the drunken brawl story to the grand jury.

Mickey naturally denied the whole episode and told reporters, "This is a crime against humanity. I've got all the facts, and this is the worst double cross I ever got. Petroff tried to shake me down for money. Burns thanked me when I turned him in. They must be doing this for publicity."

The Petroff beating was typical of many incidents reported in the newspapers. Mickey would always deny the circumstances, and the story would peter out as soon as someone lit a flame under a new one. His schedule included many appointments regarding indictments and grand jury requests, some involving him directly, but more often, anyone remotely connected to his operations. Litigious Mickey, armed with the best attorneys that money could buy, also contributed to his hectic court calendar by initiating lawsuits.

During all of the legal and political wrangling, Mickey still had to contend with local competition.

Some authorities wrongly identified James Francis Utley (Squeaky), a partner in the *Lux* gambling ship, as the heir apparent to the Los Angeles throne, which now stretched to burgeoning Las Vegas. Mickey did not perceive Utley or anyone else as a permanent threat. He ran an abortion clinic in Los Angeles that catered to women from the Pacific Northwest.[18] Perverse Utley would dress up as a doctor to attend the operations, and insisted on conducting his own personal examination that included sex. He also owned a few gambling traps, ran bingo games, and used hockshops as fronts.

Mickey's take on Utley did not include leadership potential: "I don't think Dragna realized it, that this guy Utley was an out-and-out stool pigeon for the D.A. and attorney general's office." Mickey admitted that Bugsy had once asked him to refrain from attacking Utley, citing that Utley's business with the police was part of regular activities. If that was true, the California Crime Commission was not spilling what they knew to the public.

Jim Richardson of the *Los Angeles Examiner* reported that Mickey confessed to him that he had considered killing Utley, but the boys took a vote and decided that a beating was sufficient.

"Utley's rise spells more trouble for Mickey," naysayer author Turkus advertised incorrectly. He continued: "...the noisy hoodlum and a strong-arm aid barged into Utley's restaurant to settle a difference of opinion. In his typically show-off style, Mickey picked a busy noon hour. They gave Utley a savage pistol-whipping, while some one hundred luncheon customers looked on."

According to Mickey, the incident took place in front of the famous Brown Derby on Vine Street.[19] Mickey had left Champ Segal's barbershop at lunchtime. Utley was talking to a "copper" named Roughhouse Brown; Mickey assumed Utley was doing some of his stool pigeon work, and he nonchalantly continued on his way. Utley spotted him and walked over, which didn't sit well with status-conscious Mickey, who didn't want to be seen in public with Utley and a cop.

The retired pugilist remembered: "So I went over and I give him [Utley] a few backhanders—beat him up pretty badly." He admitted that there were a few onlookers. "We didn't try to kill him." He likely had clubbed Utley unconscious with a pistol butt.

Mickey understood how to use Hollywood, the media, and politicians to his benefit. Yet Turkus predicted his demise after the Utley incident: "It is just such flamboyancy that stamps Mickey as a plug-ugly who seeks to blow his importance up to the stature of a ranking boss of the Syndicate. It is notable through the years, none of the big-shot moguls ever went around attracting attention in public, anywhere. They have, in fact, shunned all such antics. Lucky and Lepke and Frank Costello and Joey Adonis and the Fischettis and the rest—it is their very aversion to the public exhibitionism Mickey displays which has made them powerful."

Many writers didn't see Mickey's manipulation of the media and the public as a tool and maintained that he was naïve. Most gangsters, before and after him, publicly belittled their personal intelligence and diminished the size and success of their ventures when speaking with the media. The East Coast brass were both admonishing and admiring of his consistent public style. Frank Costello was baffled by him: "Jesus Christ, Mickey, that publicity is going to kill ya." Lucky Luciano always had said of the publicly demure Costello, "...now there is a man who knows how to keep his mouth shut and tend to business."

Mickey was in flux, and took personal stock of his position. He was aware that his celebrity status might interfere with his ability to make an illegal living. He still had a steady flow of cash, and his envious empire had a national following, but the recent wave of publicity cut his profit margins, and he questioned the benefits of such overwhelming publicity and concomitant fame. He craved the attention, but liked the money more.

The ballyhoo also had a negative effect on his social life, and contributed to a mild depression. When his nefarious exploits repeatedly hit the papers, many celebrities who had become accustomed to his habitual presence in the clubs, and were never shy about using his promotional or financial resources, began to distance themselves from his exploits and turn down his social invitations.

He was suddenly afraid to contact people that he had previously felt were his friends. Florabel Muir characterized him as a man who "leads a lonely life surrounded only by those whose reputations can't be damaged by association with him."

It was a turning point in his life. He became aware of the duality of celebrity. His public image, always something that inspired him, had now become a source of isolation.

Like anyone addicted to fame, Mickey could not stop. He decided to stay the course. He knew he had already crossed the line and later concluded, "I sometimes think that I've always been too friendly with reporters." He was smart enough to realize that his lifelong association with reporters and the newspaper business provided insight not available to most criminals, and served as a business advantage. He also knew that his background from the wrong side of the tracks was a hindrance to reputable assimilation. He still hoped that his celebrity could overcome his shortcomings.

Mickey continued his avid newspaper reading and was ready to refute articles to control the damage to his reputation, while he kept abreast of current events. He expanded his contact with journalists and sports writers, and became a consistent pundit.

He had his limitations, and once told Muir, "I love you like a sister, Florabel, but even for you I ain't going to talk to no cops. If I knew the killers were in the next room I wouldn't turn them in to cops."

He surged ahead, despite continued police and FBI surveillance. Some surveillance teams complained of their fruitless labors because all they listened to was bickering between Mickey and his cronies. The FBI would soon temporarily close its surveillance and phone tap operations on him. But that didn't stop the local police from continuing their daily harassment tactics.

Mickey's next year would bring him even more notoriety, while raising his public image as a local savior.

8.

Mickey spent most of his office time at his new haberdashery headquarters at Sunset Boulevard and Palm Avenue, the site of the Hooky Rothman murder. After his emotional stumble, brief isolation, and coming to terms with his knavish celebrity, his vision was to move up. He went about it carefully.

By January of 1949, the daily gross from the single Flamingo location was over one hundred thousand dollars. That year Moe Sedway would personally take out nearly four hundred thousand dollars. Mickey was making tons more money than the FBI estimated in its scrupulous but unincriminating files. Trans America wire service had folded in 1947, and the surviving Continental Press, self-described as a news provider, reported a yearly income of nearly two and one-half million dollars. It was the number one betting system in the country. It hooked up all the top bookies, providing off-track information for the casinos.

Mickey's power and business interests were now so pervasive that he often knew the time and location of police raids, which were intended mainly for show. He had some of his gambling locations customized, much like in the popular Abbott and Costello movies, where a whole room could mechanically change at a moment's notice. When word arrived concerning the phony raid, a manager only needed to push a button and all the gaming tables would vanish. Mickey had such a disappearing hideout in Midland, Texas[1] (President Bush's current hometown). The entire casino, including the card and craps tables, would disappear into the concrete floor of an automobile garage.

It was his job to keep the expanded gambling locations running smoothly and to insure that celebrities and wealthy locals could gamble at will. Despite all the public warnings, droves of suckers packed his establishments, allowing him to provide the national syndicate with a constant gaming cash flow. Most experts reported that all the games were fixed, which is more likely true than not. He had the skill to fix the casino games, mostly with marked cards and trick dice.

At a meeting at Mickey's bugged house, Mike Howard, one of his own boys, was quoted in police reports when he outlined the wise man's logic regarding games of chance: "It ain't gambling if you play gin and pick up pat hands, or if you roll the right dice. It's business. You must wind up a winner every night. Don't be a gambler—be a businessman. Get the dough, if you got to take it away from them, knock 'em down and put a gag in their mouth. You got to figure what is going on. You go to the ball game, you come back with some money...don't make a damn who wins; you win anyway. For my dough, you can take those honest games and stick them. I go to the races, and sit there for five races and drink ice tea, and bet on the last race, because it's fixed and I know it. That's not gambling; that's business. To hell with luck."

Mickey was very protective of his turf, and wasn't afraid to personally confront the competition. One example involved a tip-off indicating that a couple of thugs from St. Louis were planning to heist one of his joints. He waited for the thieves outside.

The stunned gunmen exchanged pleasantries, and then apologized to their host: "Jeeze, Mick. We was misinformed. We wunt touch no joint of yours."

He loaned each of the hardworking looters two grand for making the long trip and returning shorthanded. They sent the money back a few weeks later.

He commented sarcastically, "I guess they must of done another piece of work."

On January 15, 1949, two police officers stopped Mickey's pal Harry "Happy" Meltzer[2] (Happy Freed).

Inconsiderate Meltzer was supposedly carrying a gun without a permit. Florabel Muir, who covered the ensuing debacles in a series of articles for the *New York Daily News*, marked this per chance rousting as the beginning of a year that she enjoyed calling the "Vicecapades of 1949," named after the immensely popular Ice Capades shows that played at venues like Madison Square Garden. She recalled the incredible year: "The curtain went up on a year's run of comic and dramatic skits." *Nation* contributor and future editor Carey McWilliams labeled the upcoming bizarre events a "complete paralysis of law enforcement."

The day Meltzer was pinched he was driving a Cadillac behind one driven by Mickey. The two vice squad detectives who stopped Meltzer were Mickey enemies Detective Lt. Rudolph Wellpott and Sergeant E. V. Jackson.

Since the detectives could not produce a gun, the defense charged them with an unfounded shakedown and spiteful arrest. At this trial, attorney Sam Rummel played a tape of Sergeant Jackson talking with high-profile celebrity madam Brenda Allen, an incriminating scenario that certainly diminished Jackson's testimony. By the time the defense finished all of its shenanigans, Jackson faced charges of extorting twenty grand from

Mickey, perjury, living with prostitutes, running a house of ill repute, and murder.

Thanks to a tip off, police surprised the head of the vice squad during a dalliance with Brenda Allen in a parked car. The cops were regular customers; they would stop by Allen's place to collect bribes and "engage in immoral relations" as described by the *New York Times*. No vice operation functioned successfully without the cooperation of the local police.

Meltzer's arrest had backfired. Instead, the arresting officers and the head of the vice squad were publicly humiliated. The police force became the butt of newspaper criticism, and the ensuing grand jury investigated Chief C. B. Horrall and Deputy Chief Joseph E. Reed.

National audiences watched the soap opera play out between Mickey and squeaky-clean embarrassed Mayor Fletcher Bowron, who pledged to clean up the city again, and began a publicity campaign touting the merits of the government and police.

The ongoing Brenda Allen case (she was the target of a vice sting operation) complicated Bowron's attempts to sway the public. The vice department had consistently looked the other way when it came to Allen, but now felt that they could make a case against her. Some authorities hoped that they could incriminate Mickey in the city's attack on her prostitution ring. He went on the offensive and publicly accused vice squad Sergeant Stoker of protecting Allen's "swank house of prostitution and assignation." She had regularly paid Stoker one hundred dollars per week. The obvious turn-the-tables ploy took the heat off organized crime, and increased the public's scrutiny of the police. Straightlaced journalists cringed when Mickey accused Bowron's cops of being crooked. Unbeknownst to the authorities, the exhibitionist hoodlum, as the papers called him, had orchestrated the entire Brenda Allen affair. Even though the FBI was aware of Mickey's police payoffs, he continued to manipulate the situation to his advantage.[3]

Heavyset J. Arthur "Big Jim" Vaus' recordings (he was an electronics maven) clearly incriminated Sergeant Stoker, who bossed Brenda's operation. The topper was the court's initial rejection of Mickey's generous offer to provide the tapes, citing the source as unreliable. The recordings, including telephone calls, materialized later and were played before a grand jury.[4]

Mayor Bowron began his version of damage control, and accused the Los Angeles Grand Jury of soft-pedaling the investigation. The mayor wanted the public to believe that Mickey had paid for the incriminating wiretapping solely to have the goods on the police. The public was on to the police, didn't buy Mayor Bowron's spin, and sided with Mickey.

Mickey's future nemesis William Parker, who then worked as an overzealous inspector, stepped up the action and threatened to expose the entire history of city corruption. He zeroed in on Sergeant Stoker, who had enjoyed a long career playing both sides of the legal fence and was surprisingly sympathetic to Mickey, and publicly supported his claims of corruption in the police department. Stoker, who was in deep financial trouble, cooperated with the press, was suspended, and charged with attempted burglary in relation to a home improvement loan.

Despite all the threats and legal hullabaloo, the only arrest and conviction belonged to Brenda Allen. However, factions developed within the vice squad, and increased Mickey's enemy list. He still traveled with his own extra bodyguard, Sergeant Cooper. The FBI believed that he was concerned about his own vulnerability, and that he, as Bugsy had been, was in danger from the east coast enclaves.

Despite Mickey's growth, many crime historians confused the issue of his power and diminished his role. An FBI file dated March 3, 1949, observed that, "prominent criminal operators...have been forced to leave Los Angeles," suggesting that Mickey was succeeding. One agent reported that, "Mickey Cohen is definitely on an offensive in this area and has ambitions to replace Benjamin 'Bugsie' [sic] Siegel as the criminal boss of the Los Angeles-Las Vegas area." The FBI soon acknowledged, "Mickey Cohen is the principal criminal figure in the Los Angeles area and heads a gang of hoodlums and alleged killers who dominate racketeering activities in the Los Angeles area." However, the FBI continually ignored his national connections.

Mickey's antics became the focus of Governor Warren of California. On March 7, he released a second report of the Governor's Commission on Organized Crime, which detailed the use of the Continental Wire Service, still operating out of Cleveland, and its illegal and incestuous relationship with Western Union. Western Union distributed the race wire information to eight major drop-off points, which, in turn, supplied Mickey's bookies with timely betting information. It naturally denied any culpability, as well as the existence of Mickey's cartel. The governor asked Attorney General Howser to intercede, but he refused, despite a court order, and continually denied the existence of bookmaking.

Mayor Fletcher Bowron of Los Angeles, instead of asking city officials to cooperate with state and federal authorities, went out of his way to elevate

Mickey to a public crusader. The office of the police commissioner called Mickey, didn't disclose the nature of the call, and only said that it was important that they talk to the gambling boss in person. Mickey had contributed regularly to the mayoral campaigns through attorneys Sam Rummel and Vernon Ferguson; a call from the commissioner on behalf of the mayor was understandable.

Fish restaurant Goodfellow's Grotto, home to the Richard Nixon kick-off campaign, was the location chosen for the special meeting. Mickey joined Captain Harry M. Lorenson, a top-ranking chief investigator for the police commission, and clothing manufacturer Burton Mold, a political activist. They wanted to talk to him about a litigious radio repairman named Alfred Pearson, who had a shop at 5120 West Adams.

The police were upset about Pearson suing Elsie Phillips, a little old lady customer, over an inflated $8.95 repair bill that she had refused to pay. Fifty-three-year-old Pearson had also sued the city regularly. This included Police Captain Lorenson for $45,000, alleging that he was trying to put Pearson out of business.

Pearson had received an inflated judgment against Elsie, and with the help of a potentially bribable city marshal sought Elsie's home as payment. He won the $4,000 home for under

$26.50. Under the law, Pearson immediately charged Elsie ten bucks per week rent, which the outraged police investigators gladly paid for her.

Mayor Bowron passed down very explicit instructions at the meeting with Mickey: it was okay to bang Pearson around, but not to kill him. The mayor mentioned that it would be good to send him to the hospital, and even suggested the best day and time for a hit.

Mickey offered the smart way out, kill the bum, but acquiesced to Bowron's plan. Consumer advocate Mickey sent seven of his hooligans to rough up Pearson. Initially posing as reporters, they spoke to Pearson's daughter-in-law, sometimes rudely, only later having their "editor" apologize by phone.

A Keystone Cop scenario unfolded. On March 19, 1949, the skullduggery contingent arrived disguised as pickets and nearly killed Pearson. He suffered a cracked skull and a fractured right arm after the do-gooders went at him with fists, iron bars, feet, and pistol butts.

Two rookie cops, Allen Rubin and W. S. Carey, were conveniently in the area, along with amateur photographer Roy Diehl. The officers watched as the departing bad boys rushed into a sedan.

The perpetrators made an illegal U-turn, headed west on Adams, and the police gave chase. Rubin and Carey radioed for additional patrol cars, brandished their weapons, and forced the sedan to pull over at 2124 Orange Drive. Other patrol cars arrived; officers cuffed the scoundrels. The police found several pistols under the car seats, and recovered a riding crop and a tire iron that flew out of the fleeing vehicle during the pursuit. Without further delay, the officers issued a traffic ticket.

The seven perps arrested were Neddie Herbert, Frankie Niccoli, Davey Ogul, Happy Meltzer, Eli Lubin, Lou Schwartz, and Jimmy Rist. The list of defendants, dubbed the "Seven Dwarfs" by the *Herald*, would later grow to thirteen.

After the radio police took the boys into custody, Wilshire Bureau Detective Lieutenant Jack Swan promptly ordered their release. One of the dwarfs warned the police, "...you square this beef, or we're going to shoot the works against the department." Lt. Swan claimed that he didn't know who the boys were; he thought that they were local businessmen who had formed a picket line, and had legal gun permits.

Out of jail, some of Mickey's' Disney characters absconded to Oracle Junction, Phoenix. Mickey recalled that the *Examiner*'s Jim Richardson offered the corporate plane to fly at least three of the dwarfs to Phoenix so that they could hole up at Stumpy Zevon's residence. Judge Schweitzer sentenced a missing Davey Ogul to ninety days in jail after his attorney Joseph T. Fornow told the judge that Davey had telephoned to say that he was ill.

Sergeant Winfield Scott Wolfe had told the rookie police Officers Rubin and Carey, and traffic officers William Hinkens and Doyle Crowder, to tear up their notes and not discuss the case, and treat it as a routine shakedown, citing a need to protect the department.

The *Herald Express*, a Hearst-controlled newspaper, ran this March headline: SEEK COHEN POLITICAL LINK IN POLICE HUSHUP SCANDAL. The column head read, HEARING OF BOSS IS SET.

Mickey laughed off the whole situation. "They say they're lookin' for some of my boys, well I don't have any boys anymore." The *Express* called him "affable" in its article.

According to him, he had arrived at Pearson's shop with only little Davey Ogul and Jimmy Rist, a three-hundred-pound *shtarker* and former fighter. The embellishment mentions that three hundred onlookers applauded the event from outside the store.

After the beating, while Mickey waited at his office in Slapsy Maxie's, he found out about a technical problem—Pearson had recorded the beating. He had snapped on the recording device as soon as Mickey's boys had entered. He also had recorded prior telephone calls from the phony newspaper reporters. Mickey sent dainty Jimmy Rist back to get the device. The FBI was livid: they overheard the plan to retrieve the recording tape.

Mickey also secured the negatives of amateur photographer Roy Diehl's photographs taken during the arrests. Bob Will, the police reporter for the *LA Times*, acted as an intermediary. Mickey failed to buy the newspaper prints from editor Chester "Smokey" Hale.

The new champion of civil rights became an overnight cult hero. Because of conservative public pressure, the police pinched Mickey, and he posed for an ominous-looking photo trailed by one of his henchman, forty-one-year-old Solly Davis. He and Davis were booked separately on suspicion of conspiracy at the county jail. Bail for each was set at a monstrous one hundred thousand dollars.[5] Bail bondsman Glasser Brothers posted the money for Mickey, but Solly remained in jail. Superior Judge Charles W. Fricke, contacted at home at 9:00 p.m., signed the writ for Mickey's release.

Unshaven Mickey, dressed in a zippered golf jacket, v-neck sweater and wide-brimmed hat, asked his captors in front of the press, "What is this, anyway?" while he waited for his release.

He confided with reporters, "What can I say? I guess they just need publicity for the elections, or something. I knew it was going to happen, I knew they would get me before the election."

LaVonne picked him up at the police station and they went to dinner at a Vine Street restaurant in Hollywood. He told reporters that after dinner he intended to head home.

This time Mickey was unsure if the FBI would play ball with the local authorities, so he opted for a safe haven within short flying time of Los Angeles, and left for Mexico until things died down, leaving Frankie Niccoli in charge of Michael's Haberdashery. Mickey knew that he had nothing to fear from local authorities, but wisely waited to see what the FBI would do, but their informants came up with little, often spying on the personal lives of Mickey's employees and associates, who boasted of windfalls from the past such as the illegal nylon business. Agents knew that it would be difficult to make a case against Mickey, but trudged onward with their flimsy informant program.

Three days after the beating, local authorities asked for FBI assistance in bringing the stray dwarfs back home. Assistant U.S. Attorney Ray Kinnison had wired Attorney General Tom C. Clark in Washington because this whole episode was a civil rights violation. The FBI did not confirm the request, and therefore kept their usual distance from Mickey and his gang.

A grand jury convened to look into the role of the police in freeing Mickey's boys. Mayor Bowron and Chief of Police Horrall tried to control the situation in the media. The D.A. charged Lt. Swan with releasing felony suspects without knowing the facts and ordering the release of potential evidence without a full investigation. Sergeant Wolfe had one additional charge, instructing officers to withhold and destroy evidence.

Bow tied D.A. Simpson asked jury foreman Harry A. Larson to schedule a special panel for the Friday after March 23 to review Mickey's indictment. Simpson later talked tough to the newspapers: "We have asked that all available evidence be delivered to us...no one will be spared and that the chips will fall where they may."

Bulldog Assistant D.A. John Barnes echoed the sentiment: "No punches will be pulled."

Simpson later admitted that it would be tough to get Mickey. Everyone was convinced that he had orchestrated the scenario but evidence was lacking. The D.A. backed off. "... But it's pretty hard to put the finger on the person in back of a web."

Chief Horrall still wanted the book thrown at Mickey and the dwarfs, including robbery, burglary, and assault with intent to commit murder.

Mayor Bowron supported Horrall, but needed to reassure the public in the newspapers. Bowron mimicked the still popular nineteenth-century Ivory soap advertisement, assuring that the police department was "99.44% pure." Mickey controlled many cops in the infinitesimal ".56%" portion.

The Pearson saga continued to make regular front-page news. The publicity rivaled anything previously recorded, and the newspapers further christened Mickey and his gang, Snow White and the Seven Dwarfs. A popular cartoon depicting the gang in Disney drag filled the newspapers.

"Mickey was treated as the patron saint of the disenfranchised in Los Angeles," said journalist Pete Noyes.

The media played up Elsie-the-widow as a victim, embellishing that she was caring for her son's child while he was off in the military, preparing to fight in Korea.

Good Samaritan Mickey returned to town, and latched on to his new image expressed in the *Examiner*, a "hounded Robin Hoodlum fighting off the scheming minions of the law."

Prosecutors charged Snow White with assault with a deadly weapon, murder, and obstruction of justice. Attorney Sam Rummel headed Mickey's defense team with the cooperation of local police and politicians. Desperate fishing-expedition-styled prosecutors indicted clothing manufacturer Burton Mold for obstruction of justice.

The convened grand jury reviewed the tangled legal process, beginning with when the police returned the gang's weapons and let them off the hook without charges. They focused on the subsequent police suspensions.

Captain Harry M. Lorenson somewhat sided with Mickey: "The only thing I am interested in is legal action against Pearson. I do not approve of gangster methods such as Cohen's. I think the parties responsible for this should be apprehended immediately. I have accused Pearson of being the most dishonest businessman in the city...one and two calls a day from people Pearson gypped... We have hundreds of witnesses to testify against him." He told suspicious reporters that he had never met Mickey.

Pearson continued his legal quest to convict Lorenson for malicious prosecution and civil conspiracy, claiming that he tried to destroy Pearson's business, and ridicule him publicly in the process. A recuperating Pearson told Chief Horrall, "I may be laughing now but the next time you see me I may be in a morgue. That's where I'll be. And I ain't kidding."

The FBI informant was still in place and concentrated on Niccoli's relationship with an unnamed female in the hope of digging up evidence against Mickey. The plant reported Niccoli's interpersonal fights, as if his social break-ups had an impact on Mickey or the case. One FBI agent gingerly wrote that the informant wasn't giving them much, but he remained on the payroll anyway. Another agent begrudgingly wrote that based on what he could assess from the local police informants it would be difficult to make a case against Mickey.

On March 28, 1949, the FBI finally installed their new microphone surveillance, after several failed attempts having to do with "leased wire" problems. By May, they gave up on interfering in the Pearson case, and again dismantled their new high-tech devices. They received tip information from columnist Walter Winchell on April 18 that proved of little help.

In early May, an ambush took place while Mickey drove his car home to Brentwood. The modified car could travel at higher speeds than most street vehicles. He was under fire for several blocks, and dodged bullets from shotguns and Tommy guns, much like the gangster movies. Lying on the front seat, he managed to steer the car along main drag Wilshire Boulevard, while he dodged the crossfire. Like movie stars Cagney, Raft, or Robinson, he drove through the deluge unscathed.

He supplied this account of his behavior during the fusillade: "I'm probably at my coolest in an emergency. The minute I sensed what was happening, I fell to the floor and rode that goddamn car all the way down Wilshire with one hand. I probably couldn't do it again in a thousand times... With all the shooting, I only got hit with the flying glass, but I must have had fourteen, fifteen, sixteen little pieces of glass in me."

When Mickey arrived home, his dinner guests were waiting for him, including mob actor George Raft! Nobody was able to sit down to eat except Mickey, who enjoyed his strip steak and Cherries Jubilee as if nothing had happened. Raft was in no mood to consume his favorite apple pie after seeing his bloodied host, who, for the moment, minimized the event.

The whole town was edgy. Another incident took place in a hangout called Plymouth House, which catered to both the police and the mob. Fred Otash, working for the police at the time, related how two of Mickey's bodyguards heckled him and his partner Rudy Diaz when they had entered the restaurant. When the bad guys spat on the floor, Diaz went to work on one of them. As Eli Lubin came to the bodyguard's aid, Otash tripped Lubin and hit him in the back of the head with a gun.

Mickey ran out of the dining room, with his napkin still neatly tucked inside his vest, and yelled, "What the hell's going on here?"

Otash replied, "Two of your seven dwarfs think it's cute to spit on cops and no sonofabitch is going to get away with that. Take these idiots back inside and give them their pablum. They're not ready for steak yet."

The following week Mickey and his gorillas ducked raining bullets as they exited the same establishment. The reporters, who knew about the previous fight, suspected the cops, particularly because the recovered buckshot looked like the police issue variety. Otash had an alibi, telling the FBI that the alleged assailants had been fishing in Malibu with many witnesses, and things cooled down.

Toward the end of May, Los Angeles police concentrated on locating Mickey's missing dwarfs. One lucky search tip forced a "flying squadron" of police to head to balmy Palm Springs to search for anyone associated with the Alfred Pearson beating. The *Los Angeles Times* described how a sweep of the area took place, something hard to accomplish in a sprawling desert.

The big plans of Sergeant John J. O'Mara of Los Angeles and the local Palm Springs Chief A. G. Kettman resulted in a series of low-level arrests of ex-cons and party girls who knew Mickey. While sweeping sunny Palm Springs, Sergeant O'Mara suggested that Eli Lubin and James Rist were more likely in Phoenix.

Back in town, the nightclub scene could sometimes become a little raucous, irrespective of mob business. The morning hours of May 31, 1949, witnessed trouble at popular Charley Foy's Supper Club, 15463 Ventura Boulevard, in Sherman Oaks. Mickey and LaVonne were out for dinner with the Rummels. One of the patrons was tablehopping after one in the morning. When the likely inebriated guest starting flirting with Mickey and Rummel's wives, Rummel gave the man a good shove and said, "Get going."

The man started a fight at the adjacent table and then everyone got into the act. Fortunately, heavyweight boxer Lou Nova, who at one time had gone up against Joe Louis, stepped in while Mickey and his group made for the door.

Sam Rummel said, "I told Mickey it was time for us to get out. In a half second all hell broke loose at our table..."

Captain Charles Stanley arrived to find a quiet restaurant, a cooperative Lou Nova, and some broken glass. Nova gave police a calm explanation: "I walked in and saw a gray-haired man about six feet tall, and a lot of people milling around. I quieted them down and tried to help a couple of screaming women who were nearly hysterical. Later I saw the man being escorted from the room. I don't know who he was."⁶

Lt. William Burns, chief of the police gangster squad, told reporters that he would question Mickey and Rummel.

Walter Winchell supplied the FBI with a note concerning actress Peggy Ann Garner.⁷ She had opened in a new Broadway show in May "and Mickey Cohen, the West Coast gangster, is backing it with $75,000." The blacked-out names of the people who had passed the information to Winchell were probably the producers, intent on drumming up publicity by supplying him the information. His intentions remain unclear; the information is hardly incriminating. A personal notation from him, "To Hoover," indicated an ongoing familiarity between the reporter and the FBI czar, although some called Hoover "Edgar."

The FBI focused on every step Mickey took, despite having given up surveillance at his home and places of business. They claimed that one of his attorneys talked him out of participating in a *Collier's* magazine first-person story. *Collier's* instead ran with a story on the powerful lobbies that influenced state politics.

Agents questioned the legality of the fight game in Los Angeles, and considered that Mickey was fixing fights. They wondered, what were Mickey's connections to the local tracks like Santa Anita? What did the local specialized Gangster Squad have on Mickey? Many exchanges between Washington and Los Angeles resulted in the same foregone conclusion: "case closed...not under our jurisdiction." The FBI forever provided Mickey with a free ride.

The feds barely recognized the expansiveness of Mickey's ventures, although they acknowledged that he was no longer a local phenom: "...Mickey Cohen is presently engaged in major criminal operations involving interstate enterprises and that he definitely plans to expand in the future." The agent who wrote it suggested that they bug Mickey's office again. FBI boss Hoover granted the request in 1949, and the agents started over.

They also tried to monitor a series of Mickey's phone numbers, as if linking the numbers could provide a national crime pattern. The list that surfaced is somewhat laughable. Joe Glaser, president of Associated Booking Corporation, was one contact detailed extensively in a memo titled, "Michael Cohen, wa. Mickey Cohen." Glaser booked bands, and Mickey or his club employees had many reasons to talk with him.[8] The FBI agents checked Glaser's corporate stock registration, his banks, and business contacts, but nothing turned up in the feds' New York office.

Another report mentioned that a series of phone calls indicated Mickey's ties to organized crime in Arizona, but the FBI still ignored his national tutelage.

Information about Sergeant E. V. Jackson and Lieutenant Rudy Wellpott filled the papers again, and the public had a peek into the Brenda Allen back-story—how Mickey had pulled all the strings. Jackson wanted to take Mickey on in the newspapers. By outlining his perspective as a victim, he claimed that Mickey had threatened him with telephone records of conversations with Allen, because of Harold "Happy" Meltzer's gun toting charge. Mickey had approached Jackson at Temple and Broadway, and threatened him with problems if he made any trouble for Happy Meltzer. Mickey called Jackson a "sucker" in the matter, and suggested that he agree to let Meltzer plead guilty with a reduced penalty, the usual offer. When Jackson and Wellpott refused, they knew that Mickey would discredit them.

Jackson publicly pleaded, "If...I was unable to take criminal action against an associate of Mickey Cohen because I feared exposure by evidence he had collected, I would never have allowed myself to be placed in my present condition... It is also unfortunate that certain of the press have by speculation and inference purported these charges to be unquestionably true."

The press sided with Mickey's campaign of maligning the police, but Jackson still tried a final impassioned plea: "I ask the people of this city to support and assist Chief Horrall...," and blamed Mickey for all the public ill will toward the authorities.

Mayor Fletcher Bowron, who ran on the slogan of having "kept the city clean," was re-elected by a landslide for his fourth term on May 31. Many citizens thought that Bowron had the mob under control. The in-denial residents believed that the mob was nonexistent, merely an exaggeration of pulp fiction writers and eager journalists. Some mob critics presented the diametrically opposed view— that the dirty mob profits actually drained the local economy. Two days after the city of Los Angeles confirmed Bowron, local newspapers began an investigative series of articles dealing with police department scandals, despite the former support of the *Los Angeles Daily News* during the mayoral election.

On June 17, 1949, the FBI noted that they had been monitoring Mickey's business contacts, Oak Valley Farms, Jay Lord Hatters, Jayne Thomas (a woman's hat maker), Jay Hatters, and Jay Lord Manufacturing, a series of companies that sold "a general line of men's furnishings and haberdashery." Despite his haberdashery, and his own personal collection of over twenty boxed hats, the information on his clothing exploits continued to fill FBI files. Granted, mob influence in the garment industry was no secret, and ranged from ownership to delivery trucks, but the FBI made no allegations regarding Mickey's garment center associates, nor mentioned the fact that he utilized a loan shark bank for the garment center operated by Neddie. By June 21, the naïve FBI finally realized—again—that they weren't going to get anything on him by bugging his house, clubs, or haberdashery. The eavesdropping was discontinued on June 21, "inasmuch as same has proved unproductive." Top brass ordered the agents to destroy all handwritten logs; the information was useless and embarrassing.

Local authorities still wondered if Burbank was home to illicit activities, like gambling. The 1949 county grand jury decided to reopen the matter after chairman Harry Lawson of the Criminal Complaints Committee received a request to investigate on June 29. The 1948 grand jury had previously reviewed the same matter, and focused on Mickey's Dincara Stock Farm. Burbank City Prosecutor William Taylor had had no choice but to originally dismiss the charges. A rabbi had signed an affidavit certifying that the alleged gamblers had attended a charity event at Dincara to raise money for the Palestine war. He stated that Mickey had lent the facility for the affair. The current anonymous complainant still had his suspicions, particularly after Burbank police released three men on gambling charges back in May, even though officers found the most modern gaming equipment valued at over twenty-five thousand dollars. Police always released Dincara gamblers for lack of evidence, and confiscated none of the equipment, not as much as a deck of cards, to the dismay of grand jurors.

Mickey received a subpoena to appear at the Mitchum marijuana trial in July 1949. The Los Angeles *Herald Express* and other newspapers eagerly covered every move of the sensational celebrity-driven circus. A photo of police officer Audre Davis outside the grand jury room, replete with Hollywood sunglasses, purse, and scarf, appeared in the July 11 issue.

The newspapers helped promote Mickey's ethical perspective. "I have never mixed with prostitution or neither did I mix with narcotics," was always his stance. "I got certain traits and ethics that I lived up to, and I followed them to the letter."

Nothing linked him to the Mitchum case, and the prosecution could not produce a single witness to testify against him. The D.A. dismissed the case; no charges filed.

Mickey's joints couldn't be touched, and certain authorities spent a large part of their lives trying to topple the reigning king. On July 19, good-guy police Lt. Rudy Wellpott raided Mickey's private club on La Brea and came away with a hundred decks of marked cards, worth about a thousand dollars. Mickey claimed that he only used the trick equipment on pros who were trying to set him up for a big loss. Wellpott also found two thirty-eights in the office desk, allegedly belonging to Mickey.

Wellpott now publicly advertised his hatred for him: "Mickey knew I intended to kill him."

When he heard about it Mickey's reply was simple: "Tell him the feeling is mutual."

Wellpott followed him around; supposedly hoping Mickey would pull a gun on him, so he could accomplish his braggart goal.

Everyone was talking about Mickey, thanks to his close relationship to journalists and recent events. The newspaper love affair with him continued, particularly with the Hearst press, which liked to describe Mickey as a "gambler." He had a cozy relationship with many Hearst employees. At the suggestion of old friend *Examiner* City Editor Jim Richardson,[9] Mickey had the attachment removed from widow Elsie Phillip's home, and he returned the house to her with a tidy profit. William Randolph Hearst had personally called Richardson to tell him to lay off Mickey and give him a "fair break" whenever Richardson grew critical. Hearst, who would die in 1951, was fond of Mickey, understood him as a unique character, and suggested to him that he didn't have to be a gangster, that he was capable of running other businesses.

Mickey didn't know what to make of Hearst. His low self-esteem prevented him from appreciating and acting on Hearst's perspective. Hearst was similarly unable to recognize Mickey's incurable social impediments, which locked him into his lifestyle.

Journalist Muir was more candid than Richardson about her tight association with Mickey: "...his [Mickey's] confidence enabled me materially to get accurate information on the many headline scrimmages in which he was subsequently involved...a benefit to us both. It gave me a wealth of information." She saw herself as Mickey's "mother-confessor."

If a newspaper didn't show love, Mickey would personally burst into the editor's office. *Los Angeles Mirror* editor J. Edward Murray took Mickey's challenge to examine the haberdashery business in order to see if he was legitimate. Murray concluded that his salespersons weren't moving the several-months-old stock. He loved to needle Mickey with character assassinations like "pipsqueak," but confessed that he used Mickey just as the other journalists did—to sell papers. (*Daily News* editor John Clarke ended up drowning; whether he jumped or fell from a boat remains unknown.)

As Mickey's celebrity climbed to new heights, his enemies grew more uncomfortable.

9.

July 19, 1949, would be another long night out on the town. Detective Harry Cooper still escorted Mickey. As per Cooper's even newer agreement with Attorney General Howser, he had been everywhere with Mickey the prior week. Mickey had acquiesced to the cozy night escort with the condition that the city and county police reduce their regular harassment, which included a lot of frisking. Money was pouring in regularly from the Sunset Strip clubs, and he needed assurances that his police protection wouldn't interfere with his cash flow and normal operations.[1]

Mickey had dinner at his home with Cooper and sexy Hollywood starlet Dee David of 1545 N. Las Palmas, a very popular social companion who made the rounds.

He had plans to later meet Florabel Muir, who now went everywhere with him. She wasn't shy about her motives: "That's why during the month of July 1949, I was following Mickey Cohen around the gay night spots on the famous Sunset Strip in

Hollywood, watching and waiting for someone to try to kill him and hoping I would be there when they did."

The growing eclectic entourage spent several hours at the Continental Café, one of Mickey's joints, before heading over to Sherry's. He also had met earlier with rotund Artie Samish, the powerful state political figure, at the Charochka Cafe.

Muir recalled that she first attended a party in the Hollywood Hills to celebrate Gertrude Niesen's joining the cast of *Annie Get Your Gun*. Louis Sobel of the New York *Journal-American* declined to go on with Muir; he knew that a cup of coffee with Mickey meant a long haul, and he needed a good night's sleep. On her way in to Sherry's that night Muir joked with police sergeant Darryl Murray and Detective Harry Cooper, "What are you standing out here for? Trying to get yourself shot?"

Sergeant Murray had supposedly been present early because he was working undercover to protect Mickey from Eastern gangsters who might be muscling in on the local rackets. Murray's boss, Deputy Chief of Police Thad Brown, thoroughly milked his concerns for Mickey's protection. Chief Brown wanted the public to know that he had a dual responsibility to protect all citizens and Mickey. He went to great pains to publicize that Murray and his squad followed Mickey home every night, and waited until he was safe inside his Brentwood home.

Sheriff Biscailuz had jumped on the polarized political bandwagon by helping protect the citizens from Mickey, sometimes enlisting support from Santa Monica chief Joe H. McClelland and Long Beach chief William H. Dovey. Biscailuz never felt that it was his job to protect Mickey, and this night there wouldn't be a single sheriff near Sherry's or the Strip.[2]

A former New York City detective named Barney Ruditsky owned and ran Sherry's, as well as Plymouth House, where Detective Otash had slugged Eli Lubin. Ruditsky fared better as a restaurateur but had his complaints: "Every night that Mickey Cohen came in, for the protection of my customers, I sort of watched the place and walked around outside and inside." Ruditsky thought that Mickey was a pain in the ass, and he particularly didn't like it when the spiffy ice cream junkie showed up late with his entourage. Despite his bickering, Ruditsky knew the nature of the business at that time—you accommodate the Strip traffic or post a closing sign.[3]

Fratianno recalled the night matter-of-factly: "It had been a slow night at Sherry's until Mickey Cohen arrived with his entourage for their usual coffee and pastries."

Mickey sat inside Sherry's with *Los Angeles Times* reporter Ed Meagher and cameraman Clay Willcokson. He signaled for Muir to join the table. All the journalists wanted to hear what Mickey was willing to say about his being the target of a hit. Who was trying to kill him? Was it only Dragna? Why did he now need local police or state-sponsored federal protection?

Brave Mickey said that he didn't need the protection, and tried to diminish his audience's anxieties. The headline-happy celebrity told the reporters that he had no fears: "Not as long as you people are around. Even a crazy man wouldn't take a chance shooting where a reporter might get hit. You're too hot." Mickey's logic had always worked in the past. Surrounded by columnists with famous bylines, actors, and politicians, he felt safer nightclubbing than he did in his own home. He insisted that the only problem was Biscailuz and his nonsensical frisking stunts; his officers still had instructions to stop and pat down Mickey's men on sight.

When Neddie Herbert joined the bull session, the banter switched to the old days in New York. He talked about how his family survived in the poultry business. Max Annenberg, circulation director of the *Daily News,* "was like my rabbi," he told the enraptured audience. "He used to kick me in the pants and tell me to get on home and stay off the streets so I wouldn't get in no trouble."

A few weeks prior to that night, Neddie was the victim of an assassination attempt outside his apartment. He had just come home from a night out on the town with Eli Lubin, who still appeared around, when he dodged eleven bullets fired by two men lurking out of sight. He pretended to be cool when the journalists questioned him. "I gotta instinct for danger... I didn't even see them two guys, but I sensed 'em before I heard 'em. I dropped to the ground and crawled onto the stairway, and their shots fall all around me," Neddie said moments before the evening died down, and the Sherry's horde adjourned to the street.

The clique now included Johnny Stompanato, identified as a jeweler,[4] Frankie Niccoli, Jimmy Rist, Eli Lubin, and Florabel Muir's husband Denny Morrison (a freelance writer/publicity man), as well as Dee David, Muir, and Detective Cooper. The tired and well-oiled group meandered outside and waited for the valets to return with their cars. An *Evening Herald* reporter described the unlikely congregants as, "...a gay sidewalk throng." Muir's husband stopped to talk with Charlotte Rogers, the press agent for the Mocambo. According to conflicting reports, it was at this moment that Sergeant Murray appeared at the scene.

Ciro's showgirl Beatrice Kay, who had dropped by after work for a bite to eat, left first, followed soon by the *Los Angeles Times* reporter and cameraman.

At between three-thirty and four in the morning on Wednesday, July 20, shots came from behind an embankment on a vacant lot across the street next to crooner Bing Crosby's building.

Ruditsky ran outside from the kitchen when the shooting started. "It sounded like firecrackers and everyone hit the walk."

One of the first shots went through a car window, missing a valet attendant's head by inches.

Inside Sherry's, Muir, who had bent over to retrieve the Los Angeles *Examiner,* turned to Sally Ventura, the hatcheck girl, and exclaimed, "Those bastards are throwing rocks in here too."

Moments later Muir found a flattened half-dollar-sized deer slug on the floor.[5] Another bullet whizzed past them and struck a glass door. Muir ran outside. She had taken some shotgun pellets in the rear.

A blast nipped the ear of vaudeville piano player Margaret Padula, who had a regular gig at Charlie Foy's Supper Club in the Valley.

Cooper yelled, 'I'm hit.'" The hoods had shot Agent Cooper twice in the stomach. It was less than twenty-four hours since Attorney General Howser had publicly disclosed Cooper's new night assignment.

Mickey was easy to find but hard to kill. The shooters struck him in the right shoulder, but he worried more about hitting the pavement in his Al Pignola suit, and tried to keep his balance, or so he claimed years later.

Neddie Herbert's luck would run out, and he fell to the pavement, shot.

Dee David caught pellets in the rear and groin.

The Sherry's shooters also hit an unnamed girl in the back while she stood outside.

Muir, pleased with her exclusive, later provided a moment-to-moment account of the action: "...saw Mickey jumping out of the car driven by his friend Frankie Niccoli. His right arm hung limp, and blood was spreading over his coat near the shoulder. He ran to Cooper, the state police officer, who was clutching his stomach with one hand and waving his pistol with the other. As Mickey grabbed him he began to sag. Blood was spurting down his pants. 'Get in the car,' yelled Mickey, but Cooper couldn't make it. Then with his left arm the little gambler hoisted the six-foot-six officer into Niccoli's car." Muir's heroic depiction has its detractors. Folklore and Mickey-hater Fratianno have it that Mickey bent over to check a scratch in his Cadillac, and the shooters missed badly, but the car took a few hits.

Sergeant Murray was no help. He gave chase, but didn't catch up with anyone.

Niccoli, Mickey, and Cooper left a trail of blood as they rushed for cover, and made it into their cars.

Dee was in severe pain and Johnny Valentine carried her back into Sherry's. Waiters and patrons yelled, "Get out of the way," and tried to make Dee comfortable until the ambulances arrived twenty-five minutes later.

Muir listened to Neddie as he lay motionless on the pavement: "My legs are paralyzed... If Mickey makes it, he's going to go to work with a Mixmaster" (any rapid-firing weapon). The newspapers would run a picture of Neddie lying on the ground in front of Sherry's, and another when medics hoisted him into an ambulance.

After urging later by Muir, since the late-arrival sheriff's deputies refused to look at the vacant lot, Ruditsky found two twenty-gauge shotguns near the scene of the shooting behind a signboard. Muir also found some sardine sandwiches, the obvious dining selection of discerning shooters.[6]

Neddie and Dee initially arrived at Citizens Emergency Hospital on Santa Monica Boulevard, not far from the Strip. The treating doctors were Ray Richmond and Robert Nichols. At the hospital, he repeated the Mixmaster remark, this time substituting "I" for "Mickey." When he was switched to Queen of Angels Hospital, calls went out for extra transfusions.

Mickey and Cooper drove to the same hospital, Hollywood Receiving.

"They almost missed me," Mickey said at the hospital. He handed his "pocket change" to the treating doctor—his version of a co-payment. It consisted of a thousand dollar bill, twenty hundreds, and small bills adding up to an additional sixty-nine. Dr. D. C. Dickey accepted the money from Mickey, who said, "Keep it for me, doc."

Cooper had three abdominal wounds. The early papers said that the doctors expected him to die.

Physicians initially exaggerated Mickey's condition as serious, telling reporters that his shoulder was shattered. Three hours later he was at Queen of Angeles Hospital with all four victims. He had a slug removed, which doctors reported nearly reached his lung, followed by plenty of morphine. He ultimately got off easy with one arm out of commission and a ruined suit jacket. The *New York Times* reported that his injury was slight.

LaVonne, touted as a former showgirl, arrived at the hospital in her Cadillac convertible. When she saw her wounded husband, she fainted; the doctors medicated her with sedatives. The newspapers ran a picture of her escorted out of the hospital by Johnny Stompanato.

An anonymous call came in to Mickey's hospital later that night: "Be on your guard. We're going to come down and get Mickey tonight." A sedan came to a screeching halt in front of the hospital not two hours later. Four men and a woman ran past guards who chased the intruders through the hospital. They never reached Mickey, exited through a side door, made it to the getaway car, and sped off.

The longer-term care for Cooper was provided by Dr. Joseph Zeiler, who almost one year later removed the final bullets from his liver. Doctors initially released him from the hospital on July 30. When he left for the final time on Friday, May 12, 1950, he had major plans the next day. He married Dee David, whom he had met at Mickey's house the night of the shooting! All the victims of the shooting were under constant police guard. Still, because of the media demand for news, photographers had full access to the injured before and after they received treatment. The papers proudly displayed macabre hospital shots, including some victims receiving plasma. The tabloid-style ghastly stuff, the kind true crime fans loved, was big news, the biggest since Bugsy's murder.

Mickey announced the day after the shooting, "I'm scared not only for myself but for everyone around me, my wife, my friends, and even the law. I don't know what to expect next."

When reporters pressured Mickey about the kind of work Neddie performed, he simply answered, "Everybody keeps askin' me if Neddie is my pay-off man for the cops. That's ridiculous. He's only been in town seven months—he hasn't even had time to get acquainted with the cops—let alone pay 'em off."

The papers were full of Mickey's racketeers, some carrying bags of cash into the hospital. A few days after the shooting, the local papers published sympathetic pictures of him lying in the hospital bed. One caption read that a "heavy deer slug" had hit him, invoking the image of an innocent hunted animal. His narrow escape with death aroused sympathies in unexpected places, and his worldwide fan mail became extensive.

Three days later, silk-pajamaed Mickey was angry about all the speculation and spoke to reporters while sipping a glass of ice coffee. "They want me to sit here and lie—just to make it look like they're getting somewhere. Well, I don't lie. I don't drink... I don't smoke... And I don't lie. I lead a real pure life." The purist had ordered filet mignon for his supper; he had the local restaurants deliver all his meals.

The newspapers played up Sergeant Murray's heroic timing, and, once in the spotlight, he later claimed to have been a guest at Sherry's: "I was leaving with my wife, behind Cohen's crowd, when the shooting started." When challenged by the press, Deputy Chief Brown revealed that Detective D. L. Murray had been following Mickey that night, but not as a member of the Sherry's entourage. Both Brown and Chief Worton made it clear that it was not Murray's job to protect Mickey.

Muir had received her wish to be in on the action, and reported in the *Mirror*, "If I hadn't stopped to buy a newspaper last night I would more than likely be lying in a hospital today with the rest of the victims of the 'mad dog' gunman who fired seven shotgun blasts across Sunset Blvd. at Mickey Cohen and his henchmen as they were about to get into their cars in front of Sherry's restaurant on the Strip."

Mickey continued to do his best to manipulate the public. "It's hard to believe we live in a world of killing. Whoever done this must be dope fiends."

Muir contradicted the other papers and the FBI, which said that only her clothing was damaged: "...I was hit in the derriere by a deer slug that had luckily struck something else first, all my friends told me I was crazy to be around where guys with shotguns were trying to polish off the famous Hollywood gambler, Mickey Cohen, and his pals."

Another day under her byline, "Florabel Muir Reporting," she elaborated: "...police and sheriff's deputies have been shaking down Mickey Cohen and his henchmen...it looks like they've been shaking down the wrong guys." Muir reminded the readers of the old days when Owney Madden was shot at by Vincent "Mad Dog" Coll, who killed innocent bystanders.

Mickey agreed with Muir's passionate take and told reporters, "How any human being can fire into a crowd of people beats me. They're animals...they ain't humans."

The *Los Angeles Evening Herald and Express* was way ahead of its time when it came to reality shots. They published a reenactment of two men brandishing shotguns pointed at Sherry's. The picture, taken from behind, gave the reader the shooter's perspective just before the attack.

Follow-up stories indicated that a tip-off call came to police at ten-thirty the night of the shooting, allowing them hours to prepare. The woman caller said that there was going to be a shooting in the 8800 block of Sunset, where Mickey had his men's store. Police drove over to find hefty Jimmy Rist listening to the end of a baseball game on the radio. The deputy sheriff called it a night, and figured all was secure on the Strip. He did not attempt to locate Mickey.

After the hit, the police investigators rounded up everyone, from Sinatra associate and Mickey-friend thirty-eight-year-old Jimmy Tarantino to barber

Joseph Messina. The FBI interviewed Sherry's owner Ruditsky, even though they knew he couldn't be helpful.

On July 23, authorities also released two Tarantino employees, Hy Porter and Joseph Tenner, both of whom worked in San Francisco. James English, the San Francisco chief of inspectors, had proceeded originally on evidence that Tarantino was overheard saying in a local bar, "I'll take care of Mickey Cohen." Editor Tarantino naturally said that the whole thing was ridiculous, and that the police had acted on a vendetta because of criticism in Tarantino's magazine.

According to Jimmy "The Weasel" Fratianno, Jack Dragna had ordered the hit: "The next time Mickey goes to Sherry's, Happy will call Louie [Jack Dragna's nephew] and we'll hit him with twelve-gauge shotguns when he comes out, which will probably be when the joint closes. By then the whole street should be deserted." What sounded easy had proven more complicated. Fratianno later identified Dominic Brooklier as one of the shooters. However, Brooklier was a good shot and usually didn't screw up when it came to hits.

A rumor popped up that Frank Costello, whom the FBI said was "recently in LA holding secret meetings," gave the order to get Mickey, but Mickey denied that Costello had anything to do with the hit.

He certainly didn't want reporters printing anything like that. Instead, he played the public perfectly: "I dunno this Costello, I never met him, never seen him, never spoke to him in my life. So how could anyone say I been keeping him from muscling in on my territory?"[7]

Edward Johnson, a sporting goods dealer who had sold one of the shotguns used in the shooting, disappeared.

"I don't know him," was Mickey's response regarding all the suspects and leads. "Never met him at all."

The speculation on the identities of the shooters continued for many years. Mickey figured that competitor Jimmy Utley had arranged the hit; something safe to say when his publisher released his revisionist memoir.

When stabilized, Dee David, who had suffered perforated intestines and a torn kidney from four .38-caliber slugs and at one point was reported to be near death, insisted to police that she had just happened by the restaurant, and had no idea that Mickey Cohen was dining inside. She also added that she was no longer associated with MGM, and now worked as a nurse. But everyone in the restaurant knew that she was Johnny Stompanato's friend, and no stranger to Mickey. A photo of Mickey visiting Dee appeared around the country; his arm was in a sling, and he wore a plaid robe.

Dee later told the papers, "I think I screamed. I don't remember. I was in intense pain. I remember trying to move my legs, to see if I still had them." The papers ran glamour shots of her.

Carl Earn, a fabled Jewish tennis pro, visited Dee in the hospital, and had chatted for some time with Mickey. Consequently, the police followed peripatetic Carl around for about one week, and wondered what he was doing at all the ritzy homes in town. "I'm here to give tennis lessons," he politely told the suspicious officers. They continued to follow him anyway.

Neddie Herbert, hit in the spine, would die a week later from uremic poisoning secondary to his kidney injury. The bullets had shattered his backbone. The comedic sidekick was only thirty-five.

Mickey later questioned Neddie's actual cause of death. Few close to him knew that he had only one kidney, caused by what Mickey called "secret drinking." Mickey was certain: "By the time he told me about it; it was too late. The wrong medicine had been given out to him." He wanted to blame the doctors, and would not accept the fact that his lifelong friend had died because of their shared chosen profession.

Now the Sherry's story and investigation had snowballed and Mickey had created a media feeding frenzy (years before the expression materialized to indicate overzealous and tiresome reporting). The usual political rambling ensued about who was at fault for allowing such a horrible and violent event to take place in the pristine world of Hollywood.

"Mickey's going to get his and he knows it because I told him so," said Inspector Norris G. Stensland. He had told Mickey "he was on the spot" the preceding August, and therefore he should have known better. In one of the articles about the warning, the reporter referred to him as "the little fat mobster...escaped a gangland ambush in his Sunset Strip "haberdashery."

City Councilman Ed Davenport was livid about tax dollars going to support Mickey's bodyguard. He reminded the voters how Howser had told the police and sheriff's department to lay off Mickey: "Cohen got a bad bargain when Howser agreed to protect him. Look where he is now."

Biscailuz, Simpson, and Police Chief Worton, who served the LAPD during some of the Vicecapades 1949–1950, all begrudgingly told reporters that they knew about Mickey's relationship with Howser, and all had agreed to play ball with him and reduce their harassment of him.[8]

Mickey refused to discuss the reason for Cooper's existence. "Hell, I don't know. All I know is suddenly there's this guy with me all the time."

He intimated from the hospital that the hit was all part of an elaborate plan. He could not resist his ego and described himself as a willing victim, deliberately exposing himself as a target in order to help the authorities find his enemies. When asked why the maneuver was necessary, he declined to reveal details. The *New York Times* corroborated the concept by calling Harry Cooper a "decoy." Mickey was a key witness in the minds of grand jury investigators, but no sensible person could have thought that he was going to spill anything about Bugsy's murder or the race wire.

Mayor Fletcher Bowron didn't get excited over the incident. He cited that the shooting was under the county's jurisdiction, and contradicted reports that the attorney general had asked the police to back off Mickey. Bowron referred to him as "small fry."

Police Chief Willie Worton said that the directive to lay off Mickey came from Ralph Davis in the attorney general's office. "I can't see why police should furnish a bodyguard for a character like Cohen," Worton said. He clearly knew his position: "I can't trust a soul in the whole department."

Mickey then decided to stir things up, and told reporters that he had inside information. The *Mirror* headline based on his public campaign read, MICKEY SAYS HOWSER KNOWS WHO SHOT HIM. Howser, in response, now played up the angle that he had assigned Detective Cooper to protect Mickey after shootings on San Vicente Boulevard near his Brentwood home and outside Neddie's apartment.

Mickey made certain that everyone looked to Howser for answers: "Howser must have had a red-hot tip to want to give me a man to watch me."

His corrupt mentor Sheriff Biscailuz, protecting his turf, said that he had had two men assigned to follow Mickey, one a Sergeant Brown. Insincere Biscailuz promised to follow up with his men, and find the shooters. Under public pressure, he vowed to "clean up the case," and assigned six extra deputies to patrol the Strip. In answer to what Sergeant Brown was doing during the shooting, Biscailuz said, "Somehow he got out of the line of fire. He must have ducked." Biscailuz advised the public that they shouldn't be concerned about Mickey and Neddie Herbert. "They asked for it. They sleep all day and prowl at night."

D.A. Simpson chimed in, "My office will give every assistance to the law enforcement agencies in an effort to solve the crime."

Howser further covered his rear by telling reporters he was going to "fully accept the challenge" to unravel the mess. A few articles appeared that named the human resources that Howser had shipped in from other cities to help with the investigation. At the same time, exasperated politicians and constituents called for an investigation of his "hands off Mickey" message to the police.

Howser later claimed that the hit was a result of Bugsy's assassination and the race wire battle. He said that Mickey's attorney, Rummel, had asked for help since Mickey feared for his life. He expounded on his previously duplicitous remarks: "We had specific information as to the sources which might attempt to assassinate Cohen... We are not at liberty to divulge any other details at this time... Cooper was given the assignment both for the purpose of carrying out the investigation...and to prevent, if possible, any killings." That covered everything, all angles.

The Sherry's shooting infuriated the public so much that a veterans group formed a vigilante committee to get rid of Mickey. The *Washington Star* carried a quote from a wisely unnamed spokesperson: "Mickey Cohen is merely a Mickey Mouse for the real vice overlords. We are determined to find out who these vice lords are and name them publicly."

On Wednesday July 27, Sheriff Biscailuz released the last two suspects in the Sherry's shooting, Tony

Brancato, thirty-four, and Anthony Trombino, twenty-nine. Mickey was still in the hospital, and reporters mentioned his larger room and separate television for his guests. Dr. Joseph Zeiler had seen to it that he had a separate wing on one floor, while the nuns at the hospital baked a variety of chocolate treats for the pint-sized wounded gangster.

When things died down, Muir chided Mickey about how he had felt protected around reporters. His cynical answer was, "You didn't show 'em your press pass. How did they know you was a reporter?"

Fratianno later spoke of the difficulties involved with eliminating Mickey: "I was talking to Johnny Rosselli...and he was telling me that Cohen reminds him of Bugs Moran in Chicago. Capone tried to kill him a dozen times. They never laid a glove on that guy... It's the same with Mickey."

It was true; they couldn't get him. But it wasn't over.

The Sherry's shooting remains unsolved. It was one of the most famous bungled rubouts in gangland history, and became the most sensational story of the era.[9]

The complicated year rolled on, filled with bathos and pathos of an unparalleled variety for such a short time span. The community remained polarized regarding Mickey and the police; it appeared that the majority of the local citizens had lost confidence in the chief, sheriff, and mayor. Federal investigators would not give up trying to incriminate him.

10.

Everyone had lied about his relationship with still-jailed Brenda Allen or the fact that she had employed police.

Vote-seeking politicians had to rake the Brenda Allen situation for all it was worth. A new indictment surfaced barely six hours after Neddie's official death announcement on July 27. Superior Judge Robert H. Scott charged Chiefs Horrall and Reed, who had officially retired, with one count of perjury each. Captain Wisdom, a former personnel director, received one perjury count, Lt. Wellpott, one count each for perjury and accepting a bribe, with right-hand man Sergeant Jackson receiving the same. The investigation revealed that Wellpott and Jackson had received information from Allen on gamblers, dope peddlers, and gem and fur thieves in exchange for looking the other way. The charges included, "to collect bribes and engage in immoral relations." The verified bribes amounted to nearly one thousand dollars.

Brenda Allen spoke out from jail, and threatened to "blow the lid off" the entire police department.

"I would be willing to testify as a character witness at their trials," said the naive Mayor Bowron when asked about the indictments of Horrall and Reed.

Mickey did not leave Queen of Angels Hospital until July 29, against the wishes of Dr. Zeiler, who had concerns about Mickey's healing shoulder. The propelling reason to leave the hospital was Neddie's funeral. Before leaving, Mickey paid the hospital tab for everyone, a balance of fifteen hundred dollars for himself, plus all of Neddie's and Dee David's expenses.

Mickey had arranged a local funeral for Neddie at the Willen Mortuary, 7700 Santa Monica Boulevard, in Hollywood.

Four sedans with "hard-eyed henchman" escorted Mickey to the "Jewish conservative services," according to the *Los Angeles Times*.

The first arrivals at the funeral parlor were a young blonde and brunette in the company of Max "Killer" Gray, who had visited Mickey frequently in the hospital.

Blue-suited Mickey arrived with Mike Howard, Davey Ogul, Johnny Stompanato, and Cliff Bruno. Attorney Sam Rummel arrived later with bail bondsman Irving Glasser.

Six sheriff's patrol cars cruised the streets as less than ten mourners entered "the chapel to chant the traditional El Moleb Rahamin," a memorial prayer for the dead that speaks to the immortality of the soul.

A dozen deputies patrolled the surrounding streets on foot. Two Department of Justice agents mingled inside during the service. Reporters were not welcome.

Neddie lay in a copper casket estimated at several thousand dollars. Howard had paid for a large rose and gardenia floral heart.

Rabbi Varuch Rabinowitz delivered the sermon that included, "I considered him a good boy." He mentioned Neddie's help in the underground Palestinian movement, lending both his talent and money.

Moments after the funeral, sheriff's Lieutenant W. R. Tiernan handed out subpoenas to Mickey, Mike Howard, Frankie Niccoli, and Dee David, demanding their presence at the coroner's inquest for Neddie.

Mickey left in a two-car caravan, followed by the same number of sheriff's vehicles. He stopped at the haberdashery before heading home to Brentwood.

When he arrived at home, he posed for reporters at the front door with happy Tuffy, apologized for his prior lack of attention to the press, and behaved cordially.

Deputies made it clear that they had completed their job, had no interest in protecting Mickey, and left promptly.

Mickey had booked a flight to New York for a second funeral with Neddie's extended family the next day, but when it was time to board the United Airlines red eye, his seat was vacant. "I called it off," he told reporters. "It would cause too much commotion. It wouldn't do any good to go east now." Instead, he spent a quiet evening at home to nurse his mending shoulder.

A United Airlines cargo plane delivered Edward Neddie Herbert's body to New York on July 30. The heavily insured casket arrived at Newark Airport early in the evening. Undertaker Jack Vogel, an old friend of the family, claimed the body.

Mickey had arranged for a five-hundred-person funeral at the Park West Memorial Chapel, 115 W. 79th Street, in Manhattan. The chapel secretary told reporters, "This is a very hush-hush affair."

During the period of the Sunset Strip wars, Mickey also spoke regularly with Howard Hertel of the *Los Angeles Examiner*, Joe Ledlie and Sid Hughes of the *Mirror*, and Gene Sherman of the *Los Angeles Times*.

He was also tight with popular Agnes Underwood of the *Los Angeles Herald-Express,* whom he met when she was switchboard operator at the *Record.* She gave Mickey one of her books, inscribed, "For Mickey Cohen. If you are going to continue to make headlines, please make them on *Herald-Express* time." Underwood liked him: "I get along well with the little guy because I try to play fair with him. He just wants his side told, too, and I have never known him to lie to me."[1]

Underwood invited the Cohens to a Paramount press premiere. Afterward, the entourage headed for dinner when a car with dimmed lights skidded around a corner. Mickey jumped between Underwood and the purported threat. Nothing happened, but the war wasn't over.

On three occasions, Dragna likely gave the orders to blow up Mickey's house in Brentwood. He publicly denied any connection to hits on Mickey: "Mr. Mickey Cohen can stay alive as long as he wants. It doesn't bother me to have him around. He has nothing I want. I'm an old man and all I look forward to is raising my family and giving them a chance to have things easier than I ever did." It was far from the truth.

Sometimes former employees tried to kill Mickey. Dominic Brooklier was one of the recalcitrant mob bosses in Los Angeles before Mickey arrived.

Unimaginative Brooklier concentrated his efforts on pornography and extortion. Once Mickey had set up his gambling operation, Brooklier found himself working for him. Dissatisfied, he ended up switching allegiance to Dragna, and helped him try to eliminate Mickey.

Dragna had elevated the gang status of his nephew Louis Tom Dragna and Louis Merli, the latter hardly a fan after Mickey had robbed him years back, and assigned both to daily business operations that included Mickey's elimination. The Sicilians had a few plans.

A *Time* article aptly named "Clay Pigeon" appeared on August 1, 1949. Survivor and "sad-eyed little Mickey Cohen became the undisputed boss of Los Angeles gangdom," an expression that would be repeated. It didn't take long before his competitors tried to curtail the described gloomy survival.

At two in the morning on August 2, 1949, an explosion rocked the street across from Mickey's house; the jerky *cafones* who had planted the pipe bomb had the wrong address.

The neighbors were fed up. Mickey had become a liability to his community, and local citizens complained vigorously to the police and attorney general. The cries reached the mayor.

Mayor Bowron made a clichéd radio challenge to Mickey: "We are coming after you and we are going to stay after you. We are going to put you out of business if you engage in any form of criminal activity within the City of Los Angeles, regardless of where your base of operations might be, or who your cohorts of mobsters might be." This August 4 broadcast came on the heels of a clean bill of health for the police department. Leo E. Hubbard, of the county grand jury, had said on the radio that the department was "essentially clean, well organized, and efficient," with no trace of "payoff or protection."

In contrast, newspapers published new details of the recent grand jury testimony surrounding the Brenda Allen case. The publicity reminded the public of its less than squeaky-clean police. The August 10 story reviewed the grand jury's last try to nail Mickey on his role in the Allen matter.

Mickey had previously made sure that Lt. Wellpott knew that they had the goods on him. Mike Howard had phoned Wellpott and invited him to the fundraiser for Israel at Slapsy Maxie's. While attending the function, Mickey and the boys made it abundantly clear that it was in Wellpott's best interest to show up at the office of Marvin Kobey, president of the gambling front Guarantee Finance Company, a continual focus of the governor's Crime Commission.

Lt. Wellpott related the details of his awkward confrontation: "After being there for a while it was interesting to notice who some of the people were that were present. There were some judges, assemblymen, congressmen, some people from your office. And finally, Mickey Cohen made his grand entrance. He expressed his appreciation for my having accepted the invitation, trying to impress the importance of my being there...."

Wellpott said that Kobey had been drinking and told him that they "really had something" on him. Wellpott was only then aware that Brenda Allen's establishment had its own surveillance bugs, and that Mickey had bugged Wellpott's own phones as well. It was quite the reverse sting.

The blackmail call played for Wellpott came from a young girl who complained that he had neglected her. Why hadn't he called? She sprinkled the phone call with endearing expressions.

Wellpott had also heard phone calls about Jimmy Utley and gambling games organized around town.

The lieutenant said how the boys revealed more information: "...Mickey Cohen was supposed to have records in his possession where informants had informed me as to what was going on on the West Side."

Mickey's name came up frequently during new grand jury testimony from forty-eight witnesses. J.

Arthur "Big Jim" Vaus, "electronics engineer," admitted that Mickey had originally called him for help after police arrested Harold "Happy" Meltzer on the gun charge. Mickey had asked if Vaus had any of the Brenda Allen recordings. Vaus affirmed that he had made them, and Mickey asked him to bring the recording machine, not the tapes, to Meltzer's trial. Vaus admitted that he had an ongoing relationship with Mickey, but did not receive any compensation for his help.

Mickey had told Vaus, "If this all works out the way we think it will you'll never have to worry."

Vaus had suggested that he also tap the telephones of Chief Horrall and Mayor Bowron, according to Sergeant Guy Rudolph who worked for Horrall. Vaus did not bug the offices once word leaked out regarding his intentions.

Lieutenant Wellpott and Sergeant Jackson successfully defended perjury charges, and everyone else on the long indictment list received acquittals.

That did not preclude new grand juries, local police, U.S. Attorneys, or the FBI from going after Mickey. With more hits on the horizon, this had been some year for the flamboyant clotheshorse.

On August 18, an accusatory story broke regarding Bugsy's murder. The police had taped one of Mickey's phone calls three days before the Bugsy hit in which Mickey had told Jackie Richards about an eight grand payoff with a promise of the balance in "ten or fifteen days." Sheriff Biscailuz had a fit when he found out that the police knew about this for two years. Investigator Leo Stanley, Attorney General Howser, and Councilman Ernest E. Debs all pronounced their criticisms. Mickey's attorney Sam Rummel threatened to sue. (The same day U.S. Attorney James Carter dropped false citizenship charges against Harold "Happy" Meltzer.)

The night at Sherry's, Mickey had had every reason to fear for his life, yet no one present ever picked up a tad of anxiety. He had shown tremendous restraint in refusing to mention what had recently happened at his home. U.S. Attorney James Carter broke the agreed silence and told the public about another whack attempt on Mickey with a M1A1 Bangalore torpedo from World War II. The explosive device was designed to destroy antipersonnel mines and barbed wire obstacles; it can clear a path over five feet wide. This was not an easy device to plant under or near Mickey's house; each Bangalore weighs at least thirteen pounds, of which nine pounds is the explosive, packed in a fourteen-inch-long, five-inch-thick iron pipe. The deadly goomba muscle hired to pull off the stunt had had their difficulties; the device never exploded.

Had it gone off, the house and everything in it would have been flattened.

Shortly before his murder at Sherry's, Neddie Herbert had discovered something fishy at Mickey's house. He asked wiretap expert Vaus, "Did you leave a funny wire under Cohen's bedroom?"

Vaus clipped off a piece of wire that led to a hole in Mickey's bedroom screen. He lit a match to it, and it ignited. He traced the rest of the fuse to the Bangalore and dismantled it, but could not tell if someone had already tried to detonate the bomb.

District Attorney William Simpson, who had cooperated in keeping quiet about the bomb until now, challenged Mickey to come in and discuss all his recent problems. He claimed that he had recordings of Mickey discussing national gambling deals, his relationships to movie stars, Bugsy, and Frank Costello. What irritated him is that he knew that Mickey had copies of the same recordings, and he even told reporters that Mickey had likely paid twenty thousand dollars for them. Nothing came of Simpson's public posturing.

A memo dated August 22, 1949, dismissed any reason for the FBI to increase its involvement in Los Angeles organized crime, particularly anything related to Mickey. "I wanted you to know that I have personally made a survey of the situation and have determined that there is no information indicating a violation of Federal law within this Bureau's investigative jurisdiction. This Bureau can and will not be brought into this investigation in the absence of an appropriate basis for such investigation."

J. Edgar Hoover sent the memo to the attorney general, signed only as the Director of the FBI.[2]

Another message from Hoover, this time to a local agent, stated that the agent should not be concerned about Mickey's asking for the repayment of a thirty-thousand-dollar gambling debt. Someone in West Palm Beach, Florida, owed the money, and since there was no evidence of a threat, it wasn't an extortion problem. Hoover essentially had told the agent to leave Mickey alone.

The FBI received an invitation by telegram on August 23 to help get rid of Mickey: "Vigilantes respectfully requests your participation at citizens mass meeting Patriotic Hall, 8 PM. Thursday August 25th. Please wire." The agents had filled dance cards, and declined the invite. A local grass roots organization proved no match for Mickey.

Chief Worton took this moment to renew the faith of his constituents by proclaiming a "revived war on hoodlums." The big effort resulted in one arrest: Mike Howard, one of Mickey's scoundrels, on suspicion of violation of the state narcotics act. Officers also found a gun in his home. The ho-hum efforts tickled the readership of local newspapers, who knew from experience that Mickey was invulnerable.

Mickey remained adamant regarding his unfair treatment by police, particularly a claim that he had disturbed the peace. He was already upset about Mike Howard's arrest, the night Worton sent Detectives James E. Barrick, A. M. Barr, and Oscar W. Poluch, a federal narcotics agent, to Mickey's house. He was dining with Earl Brown, a famous crime writer for *Life*, Gene Cook, Ed Clark, who also worked for *Life*, and Al Ostro of the *San Francisco Daily News*. The police insisted that Mickey leave his guests and escort the officers to the haberdashery to check on two illegal guns that they claimed Mike Howard had purchased. A verbal pissing contest ensued, short of a physical altercation, and resulted in Mickey's arrest.

His trial attracted much attention, and he enjoyed every moment of it. He entered the courtroom on August 31 dressed in his finest lightweight tweeds and a "red-splashed blue tie," according to *Los Angeles Times* reporters, sat in the back of the courtroom, and remained silent while mouthpieces Rummel and Ferguson gave the audience an earful.

All the journalists thought it was a hoot, and the educated dinner guests testified that their generous host had impugned the ancestry of the police, a heinous crime. Rummel and Ferguson put on their usual show, and condemned the city and the police force, while neatly painting Mickey as a victim.

"The police department is in complete intellectual confusion," declared Ferguson.

Vernon Ferguson, a dapper man in his own right, roared back at Glendale Judge Kenneth White in Municipal Court, "This campaign of harassment has gone too far! The murderers are still at large. Instead, the police are harassing Cohen, who has been a sick man ever since and who has been staying at home most of the time."

He criticized the police force, and attorney Sam Rummel added, "The police are frantically trying to divert attention from pending criminal cases involving police officers."

The tall attorney Ferguson continued. "This thing has gone on and on and on. Mr. Cohen was the victim of a murderous assault last July 20"—the Sherry's shooting.

Mickey had previously apologized to the arresting officers at his house, Captain Lynn White of the new intelligence division, and Officers James Barrick and A. M. Barr.

"I lost my temper," Mickey had later said after peeling off a "C-note from his bankroll" to pay for his bail.

Ferguson reminded the judge that Mickey had other pending legal matters, and asked for the return of his one hundred dollars since he had already posted over one hundred thousand dollars in the Pearson matter, which was now set for trial October 3. He also took the police to task for directing "vile and filthy" language at his contrite client.

Mickey received an opportunity to describe pal Mike Howard as an "absolute angel" and Solly Davis as "too stupid to be a bookmaker."

The logic of Mickey's defense included: why can't a haberdasher named Cohen call police unkind names if President Truman, an ex-haberdasher, can call a newspaper columnist like Drew Pearson an S.O.B.?

After four hours, the sympathetic and thoroughly entertained jury acquitted Mickey. He wasn't a villain in the eyes of the public. Thanks to the Pearson case and the Sherry's shooting, his "polls" remained favorable.

However, the judge kept Mickey's one hundred bucks.

Chief of Police Worton refused to comment on the alleged harassment and simply stated, "It was done on my orders." The former Marine general repeated his admonitions regarding Mickey and any of his gang; Worton was out to get them.

The confusing 1949 Vicecapades baffled the FBI, local police, politicians, and reporters. Nobody had a handle on anyone's political perspective, right up to the federal level. Through the summer, the newspapers carried stories indicating how active the FBI was in taking care of the organized crime problem in Los Angeles.

By the end of August, FBI agents noted that the phone surveillance still hadn't turned up anything: "The Bureau will be advised of any pertinent facts developed." They had occasionally received tip-off letters about stolen goods. Still no action against Mickey.

When the FBI became aware of all the competitive bugging and surveillance attempts by the local authorities, many grueling interrogation sessions ensued. Why didn't the local D.A. tell the FBI about its own involvement in the bugging? Why didn't the FBI receive copies of the recordings? Did Mickey really have his own records? How corrupt were the local authorities?

Mickey surely had his own records. Somebody had periodically removed boxes of files from the City Attorney's office, which prompted an FBI agent to write, "...and the funny part was it was always connected with this gang of Mickey Cohen's activities." Someone in the offices of U.S. Attorney Carter or special assistant Max Goldschein had given the city's and/or FBI surveillance tapes to Mickey. Goldschein had a reputation as a rackets buster, would fly in and out of Los Angeles, and exaggerate his probe into the dark underworld of Hollywood.

Published stories stated that U.S. Attorney Carter was ready to indict Mickey based on incriminating information saved from old wiretaps, and again how he had supposedly paid the police for copies of all his phone calls. Carter now had new information to move against him utilizing income tax laws, the Mann Act (white slavery), the Dyer Act (stolen cars), the Stolen Property Act, federal gun laws, customs laws, and the "very far-reaching and comprehensive False Information Laws." He assigned fifty treasury agents to pay strict attention to the mob's cash flow, particularly its bookmaking operations, which included the suspicious Guarantee Finance Corporation. "The only solution to the gangster problem is to go into the income tax angle," said Carter. Reporters reviewed the history of Al Capone, and his prosecution for tax evasion. If Mickey or his advisors took note, it was never mentioned.

Carter denied the information contained in the articles when asked for more details by an FBI agent. He eventually confessed to the FBI that he had limited jurisdiction and essentially no case, despite the wide scale assault in the media. The best he had had was the failed false citizenship claim against Meltzer.

What did humorously leak out to journalists was that Mickey regularly made many bets from his residence, mostly on horses, some on other sports, occasionally kissed his cockatiel when he came home, and sometimes told his wife to go to hell.

The convoluted efforts of the FBI reached President Truman, who stood by the strict legal doctrine: no process existed for federal involvement in local matters. Mickey received yet another pass, and this time from the president! He had every reason to believe that he was immune from federal prosecution.[3]

11.

Mickey received his regular public attention and tried to regain his momentum in business despite his recuperation, assassination attempts, and the stealthy James-Bondish undermining of the police department.[1]

The diminutive gambler's success and new cult status did little to change his low self-image. While basking in all the guru-like publicity he realized that he still hadn't reinvented himself sufficiently, and hadn't overcome his deep-seated deficiencies. Writer Jennings once unflatteringly labeled Mickey semiliterate and agonizingly insecure. Jennings, like others who were able to get close to the emotionally riddled leader, also understood the angst and loneliness that filled the voids in his oft-joyless periods, particularly after a year like the proceeding one. Mickey never pursued a systematic way of desensitizing himself to his own character flaws or helter-skelter existence. He never sought professional help, and relied on personal contact to reflect upon his life.

Business was full speed ahead, and he accomplished the difficult balancing act with aplomb, while adversaries still preferred him dead. He coasted and controlled most of the local action, while the city, state, and federal authorities watched. Los Angeles was still in transition and served as an easy mark for the expanding East Coast mob. Even with the growing influence of the mob in Vegas and Los Angeles, authorities still viewed Mickey as a sole entity, rather than part of a large organized crime machine.[2]

His holdings were now extensive, and stretched well beyond the local boundaries of Hollywood. He still, of course, denied any complicit role in criminal activity, and insisted he was just another entrepreneur with a wad of cash. Jimmy Fratianno loomed large in some of Mickey's dealings. The most famous was the Turf Club action in Del Mar, the celebrity-driven racetrack not far from the ocean, just north of San Diego. Fratianno, Jack Morton, who was close to actor Cary Grant, and Mickey started a new business there with fifteen thousand dollars each. The purpose was to take the bets directly from celebrities who frequented the Del Mar track. The list was impressive: Grant, Mike Todd,[3] Harry James, Al Jolson, and J. Carroll Naish. In order to run that type of operation Mickey relied on intermediaries to pick up the action. Mac Gray, who worked for George Raft, was one of the regulars.

The county grand jury still focused intently on little Burbank, home to Mickey's posh equestrian playground. Everyone in the movie business knew that Mickey's Dincara Stock Farm was a great place to eat, drink, ride horses, and gamble, but nobody in the government was able to prove the latter. On September 16, 1949, the probing grand jury interviewed Burbank's finest, Captain Clark Duncan, Officers F. G. Walizer, Harry Strickland, and a former Burbank peace officer named Phil Foy. They mulled over the present investigation, and after reviewing the failed raids of the last three years prepared for a long haul.

Juxtaposed to Mickey's protecting damsels in distress, his often heinous sexual activities became public. During September, a story broke about his pervasive shakedown operation. The newspapers spoke of dapper Mickey as a prostitution extortionist who paid a harem of lovely ladies to "inveigle rich victims" into compromised situations. Inveigle they did; Mickey had tons of recordings and black and white photographs.

Paul R. Behrmann, a Hollywood business agent (he had represented Robert Mitchum) spilled the beans. Without revealing his sources—"a lot of people would be killed"—Behrmann contacted

District Attorney William E. Simpson with information regarding one of the largest sexual extortion crime rings in existence. When Simpson learned that Mickey Cohen was the purported head of the extensive blackmail set up, Behrmann was quickly in front of a grand jury. The former actors' agent insisted that Mickey ran an elaborate scam with his stable of escorts targeting eager businessman. The hookers were knockouts, some disciples of French love teacher Claude Marsan. Behrmann knew of one wealthy Hollywood figure who had to fork over seventy-five thousand dollars for the purchase of an indiscreet recording. Sometimes an incriminating photo in the hands a *shtarker* was enough for the horny sap to fork over the extortion dough. Mickey kept sixty percent of the money, a tax-free swindle with little overhead—only hookers and cameras—and the typical male libido supplied the rest. Behrmann mentioned favorites Lila Leeds and Vicki Evans, the Robert Mitchum friends tried on narcotics charges, as two members of the licentious ring.

    D.A. William Simpson, who had once reprimanded the police for withholding wiretap recordings of Mickey, had to drop the case because Behrmann was not a credible witness, and was out on bail after his own three-count larceny conviction.

Mickey was happy to tell reporters, "Anyone...knows I never mix in anything of that kind."

Vicki Evans still had to answer questions from the district attorney in New York; the main issue of the interview was Mickey's Hollywood shakedown racket. Police mentioned that she had applied for a permit to dance in a Greenwich Village nightclub under the name Florence Fedele, a specialty dancer.

She told reporters, "They asked me if I knew Mickey Cohen and I said, 'No.'"

The D.A. also asked her about *Hollywood Nite Life* publisher Jimmy Tarantino.

Evans, who remained protective of Mickey and anything related, was clear: "I ain't' no stool pigeon."

During this time, Mickey began one of his many unlikely relationships—with the Reverend Billy Graham. Electronic wizard Big Jim Vaus, the son of a minister, introduced Mickey to Graham. Vaus had been in the process of illegally slowing the Continental wire service, so that bets could be placed on sure winners. He had abandoned his cheating efforts, claiming to have given up his life of crime, and now worked for Graham fulltime.

Mickey acknowledged Vaus' influence: "From 1949 on, Jimmy was all over me about going straight. He said Graham had changed his life and I should meet Graham personally."

During the last few months of the year, Graham complained about the resultant negative publicity surrounding his relationship with Mickey. The suddenly religious gambler publicly denied that he knew Graham. The duo would take a respite from the spotlight, but their relationship would continue.

The public continued to lambaste the State of California for not having control over crime in Los Angeles. In response to the outcry, Attorney General Howser told reporters that Governor Warren's Commission on Organized Crime was "not a law enforcement body, but merely a study group." He professed to know nothing about the committee's crime work in Los Angeles. When asked on October 6 about Mickey's intrusion and control over certain aspects of police work, Howser responded, "Let me say I am wholly convinced of the honesty and integrity of the Los Angeles Police Department, the Los Angeles Sheriff's Office and the District Attorney's Office."

The difficult year began to take its toll, or so Mickey publicly represented. He began to complain to reporters about his cash flow problems, and ultimately advertised the sale of his haberdashery in late November 1949.

"That's true, I'm trying to liquidate. I'm stuck with a big lease and I must raise cash."

It was not actually possible to sell the lease, but Mickey enjoyed the publicity. He insisted that he would liquidate his entire stock, citing his recent forfeiture of $75,000 bonds for Frankie Niccoli and Davey Ogul in the Pearson matter.[4]

Honest Mickey told reporters, "I can't let anyone else take over that debt... I'm the loser and I have to pay. I ain't no welsher."

Mickey certainly acted as if he needed money, despite numerous reports of his enormous cash flow. He had recently sold the Café Continentale at 7823 Santa Monica Boulevard to Leo E. Tomcray of Culver City, a move he cited to emphasize his financial problems.

Despite the banter about money problems, Mickey pal Louis Schwartz was able to post fifty thousand dollars bail from the Cantillon Bond and Insurance Agency. (Four of Mickey's remaining Pearson muggers had gone to jail on October 13. Since Neddie died, only twelve defendants remained in what newspapers touted as a "conspiracy.") Schwartz got into a scuffle with reporters when they tried to take his picture leaving jail.

Mickey voluntarily appeared before a federal grand jury on November 30, 1949, after attorney Sam Rummel had promised to produce his famous client. Max Goldschein, special assistant to U.S. Attorney Carter, had flown in again, this time from

Kansas City, to ask Mickey about his pervasive connections to the rackets and gambling in Missouri. Goldschein had also previously pressed the issue of the Hollywood extortion ring, in which he had tried unsuccessfully to get Mickey on mail fraud violations.

Goldschein pursued his new angle. Mickey had sold the La Brea Social Club to Gus Klein, who now operated the club as Tobi's Café. Klein's sister, Mrs. Tobi Klein Prensky, from Kansas City, acted as hostess. Goldschein was acting on surveillance information he had gotten from Mickey's house, including Kansas City telephone numbers. Enemy Lt. Rudy Wellpott had supplied Goldschein with transcripts obtained from hidden microphones in the La Brea Club.[5]

Mickey naturally denied having any connections to illegal activities in Kansas City: "I don't know anything more about this than you fellows... I don't know Klein by name, but I might know him by sight. I don't know anything about Kansas City gambling. I have no business connections there and I've never been there except while passing through on a train."

Former Kansas City insurance man Sam Tucker said that he had no idea why Goldschein had subpoenaed him, admitted having owned a nightclub, and denied any connection to Mickey.

Mickey's tax returns also received a going over by Goldschein's staff, a financial roust that did not sufficiently attract Mickey's or Rummel's attention, not even after U.S. Attorney Carter's public statements. Mickey's poorhouse act may have been designed to deflect the publicized tax scrutiny.

The independent reprobate's home life with LaVonne remained private, thanks to the media's cooperation. He did not reveal personal data about his marriage to reporters. The mob also cooperated with the unwritten rule to avoid immediate family, excepting the abortive bomb hits on Mickey's home. The fundamental design of the mob system also worked to benefit his extracurricular sex life, and he continued to make the most out of socializing without his wife.

He reinforced the concept of LaVonne's independent role: "LaVonne wasn't dumb by any stretch of the imagination—she could read the newspapers and she knew what was going on—but I never told her any of the details, and she never asked." LaVonne wisely left the business to him; it eliminated any possibility of her complicity, and any time that she had to appear in court prosecutors promptly dropped the charges.

Mickey's glamorous social existence with LaVonne was the focus of a well-orchestrated *Life* pictorial. By this time, the Cohens claimed that they had been married in 1941. The information in the article is at once both comical and revealing.

"Mickey believes her maiden name was Brenf but isn't sure. Mrs. Cohen lives very inconspicuously, rarely accompanies Mickey and 'the boys' to Hollywood nightclubs."

The Ozzie-and-Harriet pictorial showed LaVonne watching Mickey play with the dogs at "their Brentwood home," and a shot of LaVonne as she "knits and nicens up." (Having children was no longer an issue. After Mickey watched Bugsy's two daughters growing up without a father, he dropped any further discussion.)[6]

LaVonne was a petite woman with a shy smile and a short, conservative hairdo parted down the middle. A full-page shot of her sitting at a queen's vanity displayed a collection on the ruffle-encased table that could have belonged to the wife of a doctor, lawyer, or CEO. Nearly thirty perfume bottles, a collector's array of elaborate crystal, atomizers, and other decorative pieces filled the counter. The bathroom had pink furniture and "the luxuriant pile of the carpet was almost ankle-deep" as described by author Ed Reid.

The dinner table was set every night, but Mickey preferred a nightclub or casino. When he was sometimes available to eat at home, dining at the Cohens was one of the hottest tickets in town, and many mainstream businessmen dined there often. Mr. and Mrs. Cohen operated inside the Hollywood social loop, a much sought after position, particularly since Mickey's connections were invaluable when it came to sports or theater tickets, and dinner reservations at popular nightclubs. The next morning after dinner with the Cohens, local executives likely boasted on the country club golf courses, first namedropping Mickey, and then adding any one of the numerous Hollywood celebrities, politicians, or reporters who dined or dropped by the house.

Mickey was acutely aware of the underworld appeal to the straitlaced; a concept fueled by the mystique presented in movies and pulp fiction paperbacks. Despite his uncouth ghetto upbringing, he possessed a charismatic offbeat sensibility that cut through any cloak of social dishonesty. Many actors, including some who played gangsters on the screen, preferred the company of mobsters. George Raft and Lawrence Tierney, who was famous for playing public enemy John Dillinger in the movies, sought out Mickey and other mobsters as friends. Raft was closer with Mickey now that Bugsy was gone.

LaVonne frequently stayed at home. Mickey slept most of the day; his bedroom was lightproof. When he didn't appear for dinner, that didn't stop

LaVonne from serving dinner for his bodyguards and cronies. She and Johnny Stompanato watched movies outdoors during the warmer weather.

To add dignity to her life, LaVonne maintained a separate membership at the Brentwood Country Club, a distant cousin to the more fabled and popular Hillcrest Country Club, home of the entertainment roundtable. LaVonne spent many weekends golfing at the Brentwood Club without Mickey. He rarely showed up, and often left town for the weekend.

Life magazine recognized the local police conflicts: "There is little effective cooperation between city police and Sheriff Eugene Biscailuz' deputies and independent municipalities like Gardena ignore both agencies." Gardena was one of Mickey's gambling strongholds.

During early 1950, the FBI watched Mickey carefully. They reported on his efforts to secure gambling debts.[7] On one occasion, under pressure from Mickey, his goons had his debtor flown in from Las Vegas in order to pay his tab—something that perversely irked FBI agents, who labeled the gambler a "victim" and mentioned how Mickey had chartered a plane on Desert Skyways, a subsidiary of Western Airlines, to make certain that the man found his way to Los Angeles.[8] He unwisely had been hiding out at a fifth-rate hotel called the

Charleston. Fearful of his position, he had already borrowed the money to pay Mickey; he hocked a three-stone man's ring, a fountain pen, and gold Rolex. Once the mystery gambler realized that he had committed a mortal sin with the mob, he inquired through the criminal grapevine about his safety. The word out was that Mickey only wanted his money and that no harm would come to the debtor. The man originally had told friends he was contemplating suicide. It made the FBI wonder why he had bothered to pay Mickey.

As an example of ongoing fruitless efforts, the FBI laboratory tried in vain to make the case that one of Mickey's checks might have been a forgery. On January 2, 1950, the FBI called off the lab: "A definite conclusion was not reached."

The relentless pressure continued. The *Los Angeles Times* reported Mickey's links to gambling in Hawaii. Sergeant Joseph Jones of the Honolulu Police Department told reporters on January 4 that four men suspected of running a full service sports book worked for Mickey. Morris Cohen, no relation, pled innocent to running a lottery that took bets on football, baseball, and basketball.

Mickey replied to the charges: "I don't know anyone operating a gambling syndicate in Honolulu. My wife and I have a friend over there, but I don't know anything about this. She has nothing to do with anything like that."

Honolulu police speculated that Frankie Niccoli and Davey Ogul were alive and well.

Mickey begrudgingly admitted to reporters talking to him about Honolulu that he had gotten into a fight with Ogul and Meltzer. It was a few months back, over the possibility of their turning State's evidence against Mickey. He had jumped out of his fancy Cadillac, and with a fast left floored Ogul, who was standing in front of the haberdashery. He then walked to a nearby jewelry store and punched Harold "Happy" Meltzer.

When asked about the incident Meltzer had replied, "I got nothing to say, whatever."

Mickey was still having problems with his cash flow, or at least that's the impression he wanted to give to the authorities and his public. He followed through and advertised an everything-must-go sale of his haberdashery stock. The highly publicized event attracted many curious fans and the usual schadenfreude voyeurs.

In its January 16, 1950, issue *Life* magazine ran a half-page photo of the outside of Mickey's haberdashery when he liquidated his stock. The sign on the store window in big letters read MICKEY COHEN QUITS! Giant Hollywood beams from the Film Ad Corp illuminated the street like a movie premiere. The caption read, "Famous for its grand openings, Hollywood has a grand closing, complete with searchlights, as Mickey Cohen sells out his haberdashery stock." Cynical author Reid commented on Mickey's purported financial woes with his own caption of the same photo: "A haberdasher named Cohen must sell his swank Hollywood emporium when two of his henchmen skip, forfeiting Cohen's $75,000 bond."

Mickey may have appeared weakened to his enemies. Dragna had not given up on the idea of assassination. It was four-twenty in the morning of Monday, February 6. Mickey was in the midst of the ongoing Pearson trial. The Cohens had returned from a birthday party at about three o'clock. An alarm sounded at Mickey's home, and he reflexively grabbed a gun. After inspecting the inside of his property, he concluded that smoke from an incinerator had triggered the alarm. He looked outside the windows for prowlers. Perhaps three minutes later, a bomb went off inside the house. The FBI estimated that Dragna's men used eighteen to twenty-four sticks of dynamite.

Mickey ran to the rescue of his pet terrier Tuffy, who by now must have sensed that it was a liability to be Mickey's favorite dog.

Police heard the explosion at the station three and one-half miles away. The force of the bomb blew a man across the street out of his bed.

One side of the "Brentwood mansion" (really only seven or eight rooms) was completely demolished. The downward force of the dynamite left a six-by-three hole in the foundation of the house. The roof was gone, along with Mickey's flashy wardrobe. The front door had split down the middle.

Fortunately, Mickey had a modern view of marriage; his wife LaVonne had her bedroom and lavish dressing area—Mickey bragged that he had shelled out twenty-five thousand dollars for it—on the other side of the house. The separate bedroom arrangement saved his life, because when the dynamite exploded he was on LaVonne's side of the house. The entire house would have blown up if not for a specially constructed vault inside the foundation. Dragna's crew had not investigated the house design thoroughly before planting the dynamite.

Sergeant R. W. Killion of the West Los Angeles Police Department told reporters, "If Cohen had been in the front bedroom it probably would have killed him." Mickey remained inordinately lucky. The only report of a casualty was the daughter of a neighbor who suffered cuts from the flying glass. Nobody in the house was hurt, including Tuffy and the maid Kathryn Jones, who had put in a hysterical phone call to the police.

Tuffy had left his miniature bed, a copy of Mickey's, the moment Mickey moved to the other side of the house. Tuffy did suffer some emotional damage, not unlike any transplanted New Yorker. His former owner, manufacturer Samuel J. Kaufman, phoned Tuffy regularly to encourage him about adjusting to the West Coast. Tuffy never did return to Manhattan, despite the traumatic episode.

The police questioned Joe Sica, then under indictment for narcotics charges, and Salvatore Piscopo. The FBI knew that it was a routine roust. Satisfied, the police quickly released the naughty locals. By this time, Sica had developed his own national reputation. Mickey's friend, *Washington Post* columnist Drew Pearson, in "The Washington Merry-Go-Round," described how Sica rose from Mickey's bodyguard to "Southern California's No. 1 hoodlum." Sica ran his own haberdashery "under the sovereignty of good-natured Sheriff Gene Biscailuz, rather than the tougher Los Angeles police." He also operated a health club that was a "blind" for his bookie operations. Pearson went as far as to say that Sica, "narcotics king," had taken Mickey's place as the star hood in town.

Police also arrested James Basil Modica and Martin Fenster, but couldn't connect them to the bombing. They were held instead on suspicion of violating the Deadly Weapons Act, since the police had found bomb construction materials in their possession. Police cracked down on Dragna's mob, and arrested Max Shaman's brother Moe on a misdemeanor charge. They could not find Jack Dragna, now fifty-five; authorities suspected that he had taken a banana boat to Nicaragua. The roust continued with his twenty-six-year-old son Frank Paul, and Jack's brother Tom, sixty-one. Police then arrested Girolamo Admao, Dragna's banana trade partner.

Assistant City Attorney Perry Thomas had warned Frank Paul to register as a sex offender, and cited him for a misdemeanor. Police suspected that Moe Shaman was in on the bombing of Mickey's home. To the dismay of William A. Smith, (chair of the Board of Supervisors and who pushed for a showdown with Admiral William Standley, the retired chair of the governor's Commission on Organized Crime), none of the arrests resulted in anything consequential.

Florabel Muir, like many others, did not take the event as casually as Mickey. She was up for the two days following the hit, and with Joe Ledlie of the *Mirror* conducted a progressive live radio show from Mickey's den. The journalists assured the local residents that the bombing was an isolated incident and not the beginning of another gang war. Muir also reported the news on her own afternoon television show that aired on KFI.⁹

Mickey made the most of these episodes. He was always available for interviews, which fueled his rivals' jealousy of his success and apparent immortality. He even wrote his neighbors a lengthy letter, editing out expressions like "nobles oblige" [*sic*], which he had picked up from Muir's husband Denny Morrison.

On Monday morning, my home was bombed. Though this outrage constituted a great threat to my wife and my neighbors and has deprived me of the sense of security and sanctuary that every man feels when he steps across his home doorstep, it didn't make me nearly as unhappy as the action, today, of some of my neighbors...those who are trying to push me out of the community. Guided as I was by the kindly statements of those in the neighborhood who apparently took only into consideration the fact that Mrs. Cohen and I are going through a very rugged and painful period of our lives, I took it for granted that if I could expect no breaks from the mad beast who bombed me I would certainly have no reason to fear hurt from my neighbors, whom I have never molested in any way. In fact, I still have faith in them, I still feel that they will respond to the logic of the situation, and the human factors involved. I feel sure that they are aware that despite much adverse newspaper publicity not one single iota of proof has been brought forward that would show that I have done anything to draw the kind of savagery that occurred last Monday morning, and before. I am hopeful that some of the more well-informed are aware that I have done nothing in self-defense... though the opportunities were open to me...that would endanger my neighbors in any way. I have even sent away friends who would have stood by to help me. I did not want to incur the possibility of wrong and unsavory appearances. I have confidence that most clear-thinking people will realize that my position has been well represented. In the words of some of the wild-eyed characters who have written about me for the public, you have been 'bum-steered' and I have been 'bum-rapped.' Let's both stop being victimized. I am a gambler and a betting commissioner; no more, no less. I'm not a mobster, a gunman, or a thug. I leave such antics to Mr. George Raft and Mr. Humphrey Bogart, who make money at it, or to be certain other local actors—bad actors—who make the penitentiary at it, ultimately. I am not in the dynamiting business, the shooting business, or in any of the other varied forms of homicide. I sell shirts and ties, and sometimes I make a bet or two. That's being on the level with you. I would like to go on living quietly amongst you...if for no other reason than that if I were to go elsewhere the same situation might arise, if there were enough intolerant people in that community. I have faith that the regular authorities will take steps to prevent any possible recurrence of Monday's incident. And I have faith that most of my neighbors will go along with me in this belief, as they will with me in my desire and determination to preserve my home. And if for no other reason, I believe that my neighbors will stand by my right to live in Brentwood because to do otherwise would be to play into the hands of the fiends who lit that fuse last Monday morning... I don't think anyone in this little community of ours wants to give them that satisfaction.

The letter was signed, "Very sincerely, your neighbor, Mickey Cohen."
While playing gin rummy with Johnny Stompanato and Joe Ledlie a few nights later, Mickey finally let Stompanato win a hand.
Stompanato was mystified and asked, "Why did you do that?"

Mickey made Ledlie's jaw drop with, "Noblesse oblige."

When Stompanato queried his educated boss he received, "Something a peasant like you wouldn't understand."

Some neighbors initially complained about the bombing, particularly actor Dean Jagger. Mickey eventually sent Jagger a funny telegram: "...Let's hope no further bombings will knock your little gold statue off the mantel." It amused Jagger enough to let Hedda Hopper print the exchanges, but things did not quiet down in the upscale neighborhood.[10]

The humorless Brentwood Terrace Property Owners Association sent a letter to the City Council: "The presence of Mickey Cohen in this neighborhood represents a continuous and increasing hazard to life and property, and constitutes a menace which we can no longer tolerate...immediate steps be taken to eliminate this menace." The group warned the city that they wouldn't give up easily, and that Mickey should be declared a "public nuisance."

Mickey remained nonplused by the whole event, even when reminded that this had been the sixth attempt on his life in three years. "Even in those days I slept very well. A lot of people wuz, er, were, wondering if I were in my correct mind."

On Tuesday, February 7, Governor Warren claimed that Mickey knew who had bombed the house and said, "...knows as well who is trying to kill him that way as he knows the address of his home."

Mickey replied, "I'm too small a guy to get involved with any discussions with the governor of the State of California."

Repairs started on the house, attracting hundreds of people who watched the contractors work. Police Chief Worton ordered twenty-four-hour patrols. He made a point that the protection was for the citizens and not the Cohens.

The ongoing Pearson trial—still in Mickey's life after what seemed like an eternity of assassination attempts, fights with the police and city, prostitution stings, and courtroom appearances—revealed that Alfred Pearson's less than desirable reputation extended to his family. Mrs. Hazel Pearson, his daughter-in-law who had worked in the Adams Blvd. shop for seven years, called Pearson a gyp artist.

On February 9, Hazel Pearson answered attorney Rummel directly, "I've never really liked the man."

In court, sign painter Roy L. Wolford described how Rist had ordered the decoy picket signs needed to traipse around the Pearson shop. Wolford displayed the red, white, and blue signs that read, DO NOT PATRONIZE THIS RADIO STORE. HE TAKES WIDOW'S HOMES FOR $8 BILLS.

The trial uncovered "startling" information: Mickey met almost every night at the 8800 Sunset Boulevard haberdashery with James Rist, David Ogul, Harold Meltzer, Louis Schwartz, Edward Herbert, and Frankie Niccoli.

"Some nights a few might be missing. Other nights a few others would be added," wrote a diligent *Los Angeles Times* reporter.

The infamous group would sneak off to a lavish dinner in either Beverly Hills or West Hollywood. The list of trendy and expensive eateries included Ciro's, Romanoff's, King's, Sherry's, and the Continentale. Hardly the greasy spoon choices of someone short on dough.

The Pearson saga finally ended and the jury acquitted Mickey on March 7, 1950, one year after its inception. The police never reinstated the suspended Pearson cops, but their acquittals held up.[11]

Mickey still could not recoup the bail money associated with his gang, since he couldn't prove that any of the muggers who had disappeared were dead. When Niccoli and Ogul vanished, the city had permanently pocketed the money.

"There just ain't no justice," said Mickey.

Bill Howard, another Mickey pal, suspiciously disappeared in the ocean; Mickey forfeited another twenty-five hundred in bail money.

Mickey never balked about the money: "I knew they were six feet under."

Chief Worton disagreed and claimed that he knew that Niccoli and Ogul were in Chihuahua City, Mexico, and had been seen crossing the border into El Paso. Niccoli had dyed his hair blond and used a device to enlarge his nostrils, popular amongst those on the lam.

Mickey's reply: "Anyone that wants to bet they are [in Mexico] can get 10-to-1 from me." Several reports said that four of Dragna's men likely strangled Niccoli after he refused to jump ship and work for Dragna. Niccoli was not afraid to tell Dragna, "I love the guy," referring to Mickey, who later claimed that Dragna's men had gunned down Niccoli and Ogul, and buried them in a lime pit, making all the investigations and speculation a waste of time.

Mickey died quietly in his sleep on Thursday, July 29, 1976 just weeks before the end of his last parole. Some references cite a coronary as the cause of death, likely secondary to his deteriorating bout with cancer. He had outlived most of the Gangster Squad and the rival mobsters who pursued him.

Chapter Notes

Chapter 1

[1]. Two hundred years earlier the Los Angeles Basin was a plain filled by swamps. Long occupied by the Gabrieleno Indians, the Spanish took over easily; later, the Mexicans ruled. Sunset Boulevard was part of homesteads that stretched for miles. In 1850, the city consisted of twenty-eight square miles. The rich families, Mulhollands and Dohenys, owned most of the sprawling property in the early part of the twentieth century. The entire area known as Hollywood was mostly citrus orchards planted by migrant workers. When the movie business took over, studios sprang up, some by luminaries like D. W. Griffith.

[2]. Bully Luft, who started as an agent, picked a fight with CBS Harvard attorney Charles Straus in Romanoff's. That night Straus was with a current beauty queen from Sweden. He politely asked Luft not to approach the table. Luft started a fistfight with Straus, who tore Luft's suit jacket down around his arms. Straus sought first aid for his bloody nose in the middle of the night by ringing his brother's doorbell, and asked for ice. "One night Sid Luft, Judy Garland's husband, got so drunk that he brushed a row of books off Bogart's bookcase, climbed into the empty shelf, and passed out. The next morning Bogie called me at home and said, 'What the hell am I going to do with Luft? He is still in that bookcase!' I told him, 'Let him sleep it off, he's a frustrated bookend, I guess'"— James Bacon. "He once tried to punch Don Rickles

for insulting him during his nightclub act. Rickles taunted, 'Laugh it up, Sid! Judy has written you out of the will!'"—Bacon. An enraged Luft stormed the stage, but security guards hauled him back to his seat. One night Luft tried to beat up a nosy reporter who spotted him washing away his grief.

3. Mickey incorrectly cites the Boyle Heights timeline, which encouraged crime historians to link the sheriff and Mickey as children. They likely never crossed paths until years later. Biscailuz was born on March 12, 1883, about thirty years before Mickey. He started life in a home with a huge garden and indigenous California eucalyptus and pepper trees. The neighborhood houses looked more like New England than Southern California, with big bay windows, verandas, colored fanlights, and tall iron fences. The two men could not have had origins that are more different; they shared the ability to control large groups of men, while manufacturing a public image that would serve their business and political interests. Biscailuz rose from bookseller to the most famous sheriff of Los Angeles County, with a record fifty-one consecutive years of service. He became an on-camera consultant to television shows like Jack Webb's *Dragnet*. (Webb cut Mickey anecdotes from his book, just prior to publication.) The sheriff liked to ride palominos in the Pasadena Rose Parade, and dressed to the nines in an authentic costume on a horse laden with silver. "Eugene Biscailuz is an institution in Southern California and the citizens are as proud of him as of any of the

landmarks in this fabulous country. Eugene Biscailuz, an aristocrat to his fingertips, a competent executive, a courageous law enforcement officer, knows every inch of his empire, Los Angeles County, and is the connecting link between the picturesque pueblo of the past and the great, sprawling industrial center of the present. He is one of the best loved men Southern California has ever known"— Erle Stanley Gardner. Biscailuz once accepted a $5,000 gift from oil man Edward L. Doheny in order to help prisoners who were released from custody—by giving them tobacco and candy. He was quick to point out that all the money went into the project.

4. Until 1937, when he left for Reno, John Harrah, and his son Bill, famous for their casino empire, operated several of the seemingly legal bingo and modified gambling operations in popular Venice Beach.

5. When Mickey set up shop in Los Angeles, Dragna (Anthony Rizzoti), was already a well-known figure and had the police and local officials in his pocket. Stocky, with thick lips and a wide nose, Dragna had received orders through Joe Adonis, a New York hood who became one of the national powers in organized crime, to watch Bugsy, and rightly so. Dragna felt secure in his belief that he had the full imprimatur of Tony Accardo from Chicago, who took over when Al Capone went to prison. Nemesis Dragna enjoyed a mixed reputation as he spiraled upward through the Sicilian ranks after 1914, only six years following his arrival in California with his brother Tom. A 1915 conviction for extortion and

three years in San Quentin secured his position as a leader. He embraced the Unione Siciliano, a Black Hand variety, small-town, old-fashioned organization. His business umbrella embraced a variety of illegal activities, protected by a front called the Italian Protective League, organized during Prohibition. He was a member of the Grand Council, the Sicilian insider's club. The Board of Directors begrudgingly accepted Bugsy, a position relegated to non-Sicilians. The outwardly friendly gesture never fooled Mickey. Joe "Iron Man" Ardizonne was originally second in command, and succeeded in running the local Cosa Nostra. He disappeared on October 15, 1931, likely a hit designed by Dragna, who already had the backing of the local Sicilians. With his position solidified, Dragna built the Los Angeles operation through his connections with the entertainment business. He held the dubious distinction of being the only mob boss in town to serve on a national advisory commission to the fledgling industry. Gambling and loan sharking were the underlying backbone of Dragna's operation, and provided a steady cash flow. He ran a rough business, threatened smalltime operators for a piece of the action, and like all Mafiosi had plenty of legitimate business interests: a ranch, a nearly 600-acre vineyard in Puente, California, a banana business, a winery, and a fleet of tankers. Al Guasti, of the Los Angeles County Sheriff's Department, supported Dragna's efforts.

6. Lucky Luciano dressed impeccably, had a shock of wavy hair, and preferred silk underwear like Mickey. He was a constant gambler who enjoyed

big odds, big stakes, and the ladies. Nevertheless, he mostly managed to operate and travel under the radar of authorities and journalists. He was a member of the original "Big Seven" bootlegging monopoly, which included the forceful Bugsy-Meyer Lansky connection, Longie Zwillman, King Solomon, Danny Walsh, and Cy Nathanson. His close friends were Joey Adonis, Lansky, Jimmy Hines, Frank Costello, and Lepke. He died of a massive heart attack on January 26, 1962, at the Naples airport moments after greeting his biographer. Luciano, sixty-five, had lived a peaceful life in Naples since his deportation sixteen years earlier. He had always harbored hopes for a return from exile.

7. Dragna and Johnny Rosselli had previously operated the Monfalcone, a luxurious floating casino with entertainment and a sports book. Water taxis took the well-heeled patrons out to the ship, until it burned down in 1930. Rosselli would move on to be the point man in Vegas for Sam "Momo" Giancana, and an associate of Mickey's.

8. "I knew half the movie people in this town on a first-name basis. Jack Warner, Harry Cohn, Sam Goldwyn, Joe Schenck, Clark Gable, George Raft, Jean Harlow, Gary Cooper. Shit, I even knew Charlie Chaplin. I knew them all and enjoyed their company"—Jimmy Aladena "The Weasel/Doctor Schwartz" Fratianno.

9. Louis B. Mayer, like many moguls, relied on California State dealmaker Artie Samish. "I have known Arthur Samish for some twenty years. During this time I have always found his two

outstanding characteristics to be loyalty and truthfulness"—Louis B. Mayer.

10. "Prince" Mike Romanoff—he claimed to be royalty from Russia—and wife Gloria held court at their palatial restaurant. Humphrey Bogart was one of their famous regulars. Sinatra was a close pal. Bogart had invested in Romanoff's, and would joke to Sinatra that nobody had ever bought him a drink. Mike was a former pants-presser from New York named Harry Gerguson. "Mike went to Hollywood where fake royalty is as good as any other… An amusing imposter with an Oxford accent"—Jack Lait. Romanoff ended his restaurant career in a failed Palm Springs venture ironically called "Romanoff's on the Rocks."

11. "Los Angeles is a metropolitan country. There are suave, steely-eyed individuals who would like to prey upon the wealth of Hollywood"—Erle Stanley Gardner.

12. American theater included the names Fanny Brice, Al Jolson, Sophie Tucker, Milton Berle, Ben Blue, Jack Benny, Eddie Cantor, George Burns, Ted Lewis, and Bennie Fields. "How are we to explain this explosion of popular talent among the immigrant Jews? The immediate Yiddish past offered some models—the badkhn, the jester, the fiddler, the stage comedian—but while providing sources of material, these figures were not nearly so consequential in old-country Jewish life as the entertainers were to become in America"—Irving Howe. The Jewish theater chains included, Klaw and Erlanger, Balaban, Orpheum, Schenck, Loew, and Zukor—all engulfed by the growing movie business.

13. Billie Gray's Bandbox was a hot spot; comedian Buddy Hackett honed his Chinese waiter routine there.
14. Bugsy also had a need for recognition and social popularity, and sought out international social contacts. He swiftly became a local celebrity under the tutelage of the café society Countess Dorothy DiFrasso (his hostess in Italy), daughter of Bertrand Taylor, a New Jersey millionaire. New York hotelier James McKinley had introduced him to the Countess. With a million-dollar trust fund, the fun-loving Countess-by-marriage gave lavish Hollywood parties attended by Gary Cooper and Cary Grant. Bugsy and Countess di Frasso once sailed for two months aboard the *Metha Nelson*, the 150-foot ship used in the movie *Mutiny on the Bounty*, captained by Marino Bello, actress Jean Harlow's stepfather. Other social links to Bugsy during his marriage included Wendy Barrie and Marie "The Body" MacDonald. He took up with old Williamsburg pal and established gangster actor George Raft, who employed his own full-time bodyguard, and at one point was the manager of Meyer Lansky's Hotel Capri in Havana. The other big movie stars of the day, Clark Gable, Jean Harlow, Marlene Dietrich, Charles Boyer, Fred Astaire, and Cary Grant all knew Bugsy.
15. "Has history ever toyed so wantonly with a people as history toyed with the Jews in the 1940s? It was a decade of ashes and honey; a decade so battering and so emboldening that it tested the capacity of those who experienced it to hold a stable view of the world, to hold a belief in the world"—Leon Wieseltier. The

Carnegie Institution established a research laboratory on Long Island to study eugenics, to justify the elimination of blacks, Indians, the poor, and the sickly. The Rockefeller Foundation and the Harriman railroad fortune also helped finance projects that "sought to legitimize his [Hitler's] innate race hatred and anti-Semitism by medicalizing it, wrapping it in a pseudoscientific façade"—Edwin Black. "The Rockefeller Foundation financed the Kaiser Wilhelm Institute and the work of its central racial scientists. Once WWII began, Nazi eugenics turned from mass sterilization and euthanasia to genocidal murder. One of the Kaiser Wilhelm Institute doctors in the program financed by the Rockefeller Foundation was Josef Mengele, who continued his research in Auschwitz, making daily eugenic reports on twins. After the world recoiled from Nazi atrocities, the American eugenics movement—its institutions and leading scientists—renamed and regrouped under the banner of an enlightened science called *human genetics*"—Black.

Chapter 2

[16]. Because of events like the Rosselli robbery, Mickey's callous indifference to other criminal families in Los Angeles, and the archaic Dragna-run mob, the locals likely nicknamed the Hollywood boys the Mickey Mouse Mafia. Many people thought it had something to do with Walt Disney, particularly when his famous black rodent became the talk of the town, or the later proximity to Disneyland, or Mickey's own first

name and diminutive stature. (Some later credit Los Angeles police chief Daryl Gates' 1984 Operation Lightweight for coining the phrase Mickey Mouse Mafia.) When Dragna was in power, the West Coast operation utilized an unorganized methodology that was perhaps three decades behind the rest of the country, and Mickey Mouse Mafia remains a convenient term to excuse decades of sloppy mob-controlled activities.

17. Geisler was born in Iowa, and relocated in California to attend USC Law School. He once chaired the California Horse Racing Board. He defended Robert Mitchum on marijuana charges; represented Shelley Winters when she sued Vittorio Gassman for divorce; Zsa Zsa Gabor against husband George Sanders; Marilyn Monroe when she dumped Joltin' Joe; Barbara Hutton against Cary Grant; Busby Berkeley; Edward G. Robinson; Charlie Chaplin on morals charges; the stripper Lili St. Cyr; Greta Garbo; and Errol Flynn. "...in every one of them [cases] he knew in advance what the prosecutors knew and a lot of other things they had never heard about. I have never seen him taken by surprise"—Florabel Muir. Mickey always remained close with Geisler and his wife Ruth, whom Mickey described as a heavy drinker. "I have long been aware of the fact that 'Get me Geisler' has become a gag used by a husband when he is in the doghouse for some minor domestic offense which has riled his wife. I suppose that an attorney can't take part in as many trials of national interest as I've been involved in without becoming a household word, but this fact really hit me for the first time when Ingrid Bergman's divorce from Dr. Lindstrom

was racing the stork"—Jerry Geisler. Geisler died in 1962 after two prior heart attacks in 1959 and 1960.

[18]. Bugsy muscled in on the Agua Caliente racetrack in Tijuana, a welcome sign of good times to come for the Hollywood crowd and its forever wannabe followers. He christened a greyhound track with dapper don Johnny Rosselli. When his relationship with Rosselli and the movie moguls solidified, Bugsy, together with Mickey, controlled the International Alliance of Theatrical Stage Employees. Simple extortion schemes regularly bilked the studios, who were afraid of wildcat strikes, easily orchestrated by Mickey. Bugsy also made legitimate investments in hotels, restaurants, and real estate with money he garnered by muscling in on existing businesses. Some of the financing for his operation came from making loans to movie stars. He wisely also made political donations, including a hundred grand to politician John Dockweiler, who was running for district attorney. Many enterprising politicians benefited from systematic payments that helped pave the way for Bugsy and Mickey. Bugsy eventually moved with his wife Esther, two daughters, and a nasty German shepherd into a thirty-room mansion owned by famous opera baritone Lawrence Tibbett. The Holmby Hills mansion had a swimming pool and a marble bath. He would later build his own $125,000 house on a $29,000 three-acre lot in the same area. He shelled out an additional $25,000 for the furnishings, with monthly expenses at $1,000. Add to that his two daughters' private

schooling, their riding lessons, his wardrobe, including riding habits, and his wife's everyday expenditures. His daughters always remained enrolled in the best private schools, where he mingled with the wealthy, famous, and powerful. He knew how to play the crowd, but he didn't know how to control his character flaws. "A thoroughly arrogant, uninhibited hoodlum, the Bug had an ego that was incredible. The Mob had pinned the Bugsy label on him as a complimentary token for his indifference under fire"—Sid Feder. The fabled Hillcrest Country Club board claimed they didn't know that new applicant Benjamin Siegel was the notorious criminal, even though he was recommended by two major film executives. When club members got wind of the new member, the board voted to have the oldest member of the club visit Bugsy and tell him the bad news: he could no longer attend Hillcrest. The rationale was simple: Bugsy wouldn't take it out on the elderly Jewish gentleman. He didn't, and resigned from the club, with a full refund. According to Bugsy, "No one asked me to get out. I didn't wait for that. I wanted to avoid being embarrassed or embarrassing anyone else. I sold my membership for three hundred dollars, which was less than it cost me. I missed the golfing."

[19]. Frankie Carbo was a former hit man for Lepke, arrested five times for murder without a single conviction, and later served as boxing czar. Despite two convictions, one for managing fighters without a license, and conspiracy/extortion, Carbo would live the good

life in Miami Beach, and die of natural causes at age seventy-two.

20. Billy Wilkerson, who founded the *Hollywood Reporter* and was a big influence in the club scene, eventually developed a less-than-desirable relationship with Bugsy. A degenerate gambler, Wilkerson would control Vendome, Café Trocadero, Sunset House, La Rue, and L'Aiglon, and personally influenced what the movie stars ate. Joe Pasternak, one of Hollywood's popular directors, said that he "…brought Paris to Hollywood." Wilkerson, the son of a gambler who had won Coca-Cola distribution rights in a poker game, tried the priesthood and a medical career before discovering the world of trade papers. He drank Cokes nonstop throughout his caffeine-driven gambling days. Irresponsible Wilkerson once borrowed $75,000 from friend and wealthy movie mogul Joe Schenck in order to buy property near Monte Carlo. After a two-day binge, Wilkerson was broke.

21. Longie Zwillman had a long history with the Hollywood movie business; a best friend was Harry Cohn of Columbia Pictures. He had his own bungalow at the Garden of Allah on Sunset Boulevard, where Mickey, Bugsy, Meyer Lansky, Moe Dalitz, Frank Costello, and a host of other Hollywood luminaries entertained in twenty-four private bungalows.

22. Sinatra was close with Mickey, Sam "Momo" Giancana, Rosselli, Anthony "Big Tuna" Accardo, Santos Trafficante, Jr., and Carlos Marcello—the top racketeers in the country. He was quick to throw a punch in any venue. "I've heard Sam [Giancana] say on many occasions that Frank was

a frustrated gangster"—Antoinette Giancana, Sam's daughter. Ciro's Herman Hover had to ignore his imagined "three strikes and you're out" rule for brawlers when it came to Sinatra. He had previously gone after Peter Lawford and Ciro's publicist Jim Byron. Sinatra and bullies also beat up columnist Lee Mortimer in Ciro's, who was no fan of the underworld. Mortimer publicly admitted that he disliked Sinatra's singing, and dug into his mob connections, referring to him as "Lucky." Sinatra claimed that Mortimer called him a "little dago bastard." Mortimer recalled hearing Sinatra mouth "fucking homosexual and degenerate" during the beating. Sinatra paid a $9,000 fine. One raucous night after too many drinks at Jilly Rizzo's, the singer had Jilly and Brad Dexter drive him out to Mortimer's grave so that he could piss on it. Sinatra had continuous problems with columnists Robert Ruark, Dorothy Kilgallen, Louella Parsons, Hedda Hopper, and Westbrook Pegler. He also beat Hunt executive Fred Weisman senseless with a telephone, inside the Beverly Hills Hotel's chichi Polo Lounge. Weisman suffered a fractured skull. Witness Dean Martin denied that the incident took place. The fight was over too much noise emanating from Sinatra's table. Casino manager and executive vice president Carl Cohen knocked out Sinatra's front teeth after the crooner spilt hot coffee on him. Sinatra was purported to have told Kirk Douglas later, "Never fight a Jew in the desert." He likely gave the word to beat up comedian Jackie Mason, whose act featured Sinatra in an unfavorable light. His break up with Lana Turner was complicated, and involved all kinds of ménage a trois possibilities, including wife Ava Gardner. Frank threw everyone out, while the police acted as referees. When he got wind of a Peter Lawford sighting with Ava Gardner, Lawford received this earful personally from Frank: "What's this about you and Ava? Listen, creep. You wanna stay healthy? I'll have your legs broken, you bum...." Singer Andy Williams once successfully joked that when Sinatra opened at Caesars Palace in Vegas "A lot of the audience put their hats over their faces. There was 500 years off for good behavior in the first row."

23. Joseph "Doc" Stacher further organized the Jewish Mafia in 1931 at a meeting in his hotel room. The eight men present included Bugsy Siegel, Louis Buchalter, and Harry "Big Greenie" Greenberg, the core of the fledgling organization. The idea of a national syndicate became a reality. Stacher, a tried and true member of Lansky's operation, ended up in Israel under that country's law of return. He fled the U.S. in 1965 because he faced a jail term for income-tax evasion. The expressive and comical term "Kosher Nostra" involves Stacher. The cynical Israeli press always referred to Stacher as a member of the Kosher Nostra after a meek rabbi swindled Stacher out of $100,000. The rabbi invested in a kosher hotel rather than the promised educational institutions.

24. Dragna may not have been the patsy that many reported. The California Crime Study Commission wrote that when race wire maven James Ragen lay dying, his last words included, "Dragna is the

Capone of Los Angeles." Ragen's death was unquestionably an asset for Bugsy and Mickey to set up and run their wire shop; he naturally lost his race wire business. Author Sid Feder also supported the idea that Dragna was the Capone of the West, hardly in need of advice for running illegal activities. Authorities and crime reporters took up the Capone crack, but it was only an embellishment probably meant to sell newspapers. "Dragna was a man who thought small. The limits of his successful capers involved such matters as providing protection to certain illegal operations and then sending in a confederate to shake them down"—Carl Sifakis. He and at least two of his relatives, a brother and nephew, survived a long time despite the difficulties. "Dragna rose to the top among the 'home-grown' California mobsters only because he was the best of the poor lot— although practiced murderers, they simply lacked the abilities of their eastern-compatriots"— Carl Sifakis.

25. The competing news services were fronts for the race wire. The news services sold racing guides and scratch sheets to bookies around the nation. The initial main interest of the wire service was horseracing, and a bookie who handled a significant illegal cash flow needed up-to-the-minute changing track odds, in order to take advantage of fluctuations. The technology developed by the news services was the best available and sometimes exceeded what Ma Bell was able to offer classified government agencies. Regional bookies had multiple phone lines and switchboards. The largest operations

had a ticker (a device similar to those used in the stock market) capable of printing out race-related information on a narrow band of paper. The news services were able to keep an arms-length relationship with the bookies by claiming that they only sold race information to distributors. The wire company owners claimed that what the regional distributors did with the information had nothing to do with the news services. The distributors were dummy corporations, often owned by news service principals or their relatives.

26. "In covering the clubs I found myself enmeshed in the underworld, without quite realizing what was taking place"—Earl Wilson.

27. Joan Crawford made the rounds at Ciro's and the Mocambo with dapper socialite attorney Greg Bautzer. "…[he] was such a good lover that, after one performance in bed with him, Joan Crawford bought him a Cadillac"—Jim Bacon. Bautzer supposedly had seduced knockout blonde virgin Lana Turner. "Easily one of the most handsome…"—Peggy Lee. Bautzer dated Ava Gardner, Dorothy Lamour, was engaged to Barbara Payton, and married Dana Wynter. Porn flicks discovered in Roman Polanski's loft after the Manson murder investigations included Bautzer. Author Sheila Weller referred to Bautzer as Bugsy Siegel's lawyer. He was more a legend, and represented Sinatra, Howard Hughes, and Kirk Kerkorian. He also knew how to keep Meyer Lansky happy, and that included lending his expertise to help organize in Los Angeles.

28. Renowned Ciro's occupied prime Strip real estate. "Billy Wilkerson's stand-alone Ciro's

was a creature of his own—and architect George Vernon Russell's—fantasy. The exterior was pure early Southern California sophistication...bearing dozens of appliquéd squares in bas-relief: the scripted logo (with its piquantly tiled, comically triple-oversized C) sitting on a swirling-edged white slab overhang, propped up by an elegant screen of white slats rising from planters bursting with tropical flora"—Sheila Weller. The interior of Ciro's: "dreamy apple" color with ribbed thick silk walls, bronze columns, glass dance floor, fish pool, an American Beauty Red ceiling that matched the plush banquettes and urns that hid the lighting. "...celebrating clever people's ability to restyle themselves to their passions"—Weller. The vice squad closed Ciro's the year Mickey arrived; it reopened, more grandiose, in 1940. Sinatra, Piaf, Holiday, Cole, Dietrich, Martin and Lewis, Horne, and West all worked the room. Backward-style striptease star Lily St. Cyr caused a temporary closing: "She emerged onstage wearing pasties and a G-string and proceeded to clothe herself, caressing every part of her body in the process...more Dada than burlesque"—Weller. Manager/owner Herman Hover, former Earl Carroll chorus boy from New York, hired decorator Jamie Ballard to build a special marble bathtub for a courtroom stage. "The bathtub was transparent; it was illuminated from the inside and through it Miss St. Cyr's seductive curves and undulations could be glimpsed"—Jerry Geisler. In defense of St. Cyr, Geisler had Hover stand before the jury and scientifically show the subtle differences between a lawful bump and the dreaded illegal grind. The all-male jury gladly finished observing the testimony at Ciro's. Florabel Muir, journalist and Mickey pal, testified that she had an unobstructed view, and was not offended. She insisted that the deputy D.A. call her "Madam"; it got one of the biggest laughs at the trial. "It was the most daring thing on the Strip. It was startling for those days"—Army Archerd. After banishment from the dance floor for salacious dancing, actress Paulette Goddard crawled under the table at Ciro's and more privately and orally continued her attention toward director Anatole Litvak. Some reversed the action. "Litvak crouched, and—unmistakably to the diners nearby—performed cunnilingus on her"—Weller. "Part of the building is on city property and part on the county. While the two outfits were trying to decide who had jurisdiction, Ciro's practically burnt down"—Wilkerson. It would close after the fire in 1957.

[29]. Fred and Joe Sica were two thugs who handled the rough stuff for Mickey and Bugsy. Mike Howard—no relation to Bill—would hang himself years later in New York, after surviving years around Mickey without a scratch, including the Battle of the Sunset Strip.

[30]. Dr. Sanford Zevon, Stumpy's nephew, recalled Mickey as a pleasant, affable man, who was always polite at the family home in Brooklyn. Crystal Zevon, Stumpy's daughter-in-law and former wife of Warren Zevon, spoke similarly of Stumpy, but recognized that there were times to stay clear.

31. Bogart and Bacall liked to hang out at the Mocambo, where Sinatra made his first club appearance. Charlie Morrison, a former usher from the fabled Palace Theater in New York, ran the club designed by Tony Duquette. Sinatra frequently engaged Morrison and Dave Chasen in conversation about their spaghetti and clam sauce. Clark Gable, Carole Lombard, Lucille Ball, and Desi Arnaz were also Mocambo regulars. Gable loved the track, and didn't mind rubbing elbows with the bad boys in town. The famous radio personality and columnist Walter Winchell, King of Broadway, dined regularly with Marilyn Monroe. His sometimes inaccurate column appeared in over 1,000 newspapers.
32. Massachusetts-born Fred Otash became an FBI informant. The FBI dropped him when he publicized his working relationship with the government agency. Otash moved to New York in 1965, after the State License Board revoked his private investigator's license.
33. Drucker's morphed into Rothschild's on Beverly Drive. This famous tonsorial hangout became home to a major sports book where regular gambling clients, occasional newcomer locals, and out-of-town guests could bet on an array of games that rivaled current sophisticated Vegas parlors. Mickey's autobiography displays a picture of Harry Gelbart giving his balding client a haircut. Harry's Hollywood contacts would help find work for his son, comedy writer Larry. Harry even introduced his nephew, now fashionable Brentwood dentist Dr. Michael Eilenberg, to Mickey.Whenever the intimating George Raft appeared for a shave at busy

Drucker's, he needed only to move toward any occupied chair, and the patron, particularly if mob connected, would relinquish the seat.

34. Samuel Bronfman was the patriarch of the wealthy Canadian-Jewish family that traded its stake in the Seagram's liquor business for the Universal entertainment conglomerate and the music business. Bronfman's original fortune came from peddling Canadian booze to American bootleggers for fourteen years. That meant doing business with Rothstein, Lansky, Luciano, Dalitz, and the Purple Gang in Detroit. Lake Erie, nicknamed the "Jewish" lake, was the entry point for Dalitz' bootlegging operations. The Canadian Parliament had restricted the sale of alcohol in 1919, labeled it a drug, and sold it only in pharmacies. The Canada Pure Drug Company was the source of booze for millions of Americans. "We loaded a carload of goods, got our cash, and shipped it. We shipped a lot of goods. I never went to the other side of the border to count the empty Seagram's bottles"— Samuel Bronfman. Paul Matoff, Bronfman's brother-in-law, would lose his life in a gun battle with rival bootleggers. Some of the family relocated in New York and made the business and cultural assimilation that was common for second and third generation Jewish families with criminal backgrounds. "…they invested in real estate, commodities, stocks, and bonds… They supported the arts, attended synagogue, raised racehorses, and made generous contributions to charities, especially those that championed the Jewish state of Israel"— Dennis McDougal.

35. Moses Annenberg, another super rich patriarch, who once hired Luciano and Lansky as circulation monitors for the *Mirror*, would build his empire on gambling. "Moses Annenberg had fought his way up from Chicago newsboy to high executive positions in William Randolph Hearst's empire on the strength of his performance in the interminable 'circulation wars' between competing newspapers and magazines. Then, step by step, he brought out the first daily racing journals, and, soon after, the wire service company that had been supplying the results to those journals...seizing control of a service on which every bookie depended with the help of the gang/syndicates"—Albert Fried. Each wire service provider had thousands of customers. By using a special telephone line, the bookie had continual access to the fluctuating odds, race results, and payoffs from tracks throughout the country. Annenberg could never have set up the Nationwide wire service without Al Capone. "That Annenberg and the Prohibition and gambling mobs had interests in common is indisputable... Annenberg was allowed to reap inordinate profits and become one of the richest men in the land..."—Albert Fried.

Chapter 3

1. One of Charlie and Mickey's fighters was lightweight Jimmy Joyce, brother of nationally celebrated Willie, whom Mickey had managed. Willie was one of the top four lightweights; he beat Ike Williams three times in seven months.

2. The Jim Dandy and Food Basket labels are today part of the Albertson's chain.
3. Stanley Adams would do jail time for killing Davidian. He was friendly with actress Barbara Payton and actor/drug dealer Don Cougar. Payton, Mickey, and tough-guy actor John Ireland made the social rounds together. Payton, once engaged to attorney Greg Bautzer, also had a fling with actor George Raft.
4. During the forties and fifties Los Angeles was the prostitution wholesaler for the state of California and, later, Nevada. Farmers and miners demanded companionship. So did fancy hotel guests in San Francisco. Truck drivers supplied the transportation for delivering ten bucks worth of fun on the cuff. Sex establishments advertised afternoon nude modeling sessions. For two bucks, a patron could buy the phone numbers of fifty models, including nude photos.
5. Sedway was a lifer with Meyer Lansky, and helped set up the Trans America wire service, by supplying national muscle that competed with Continental. The Trans America Publishing and News Service would become the cornerstone needed to pave the way for the move into Las Vegas. Anti-Semitic FBI files on Moe Sedway were direct: "...a dwarf Jewish boy with all the worst traits of his nationality over-emphasized... Prone to be a snappy dresser...obsessions are monogrammed silk shirts and silk underwear as well as manicured nails."
6. When Thomas Hull opened the El Rancho Vegas in 1941, the idea of a complex with gaming, lodging, dining, entertainment, and retail

facilities did not exist. The Hotel El Rancho was the first full-scale hotel and casino resort on Highway 91 south of Las Vegas, a roadway that would become the Las Vegas Strip. The El Rancho Vegas changed hands a few times before Beldon Katleman, who inherited a share from his uncle, took over. He renovated the hotel and it became a Vegas cornerstone throughout the 1950s. He knew the value of entertainment and sexy girls; El Rancho was one of the first hotels to feature a risqué revue, a Vegas staple. Jimmy Fratianno and comedy star Chico Marx partnered in the El Rancho race book.

7. Uneducated Sinatra shared many of Mickey's habits and self-esteem problems. He was meticulous when it came to cleanliness, and was obsessed with his appearance. His germ phobia required no less than four showers every day. His baldness troubled him, so he used spray-on hair coloring, endless toupees, and hats. He always wore makeup applied with a powder puff before leaving home, designed to cover the deformities on the left side of his face and ear caused by a forceps birth. He was jealous of Peter Lawford's smoother delivery and social acceptance. His publicist Warren Cowan, formerly of Rogers and Cowan, once said that with a client like Sinatra there was little need to generate publicity. The biggest Zionist of all Mickey's friends was Sinatra. He loved to travel to Israel and donate to supportive organizations.

8. Tarantino would find himself in San Quentin after prosecution for using his Hollywood rag for blackmail purposes. Mickey claimed that he had warned him that the police were bugging his

phone. After Tarantino's parole, he moved to New Jersey.
9. Myford was the son of James Irvine, and one of the most successful southern California ranchers. On Saturday, January 11, 1959, police found his body in the basement of his home. He had been shot twice in the abdomen with a sixteen-gauge shotgun and once in the right temple with a twenty-two-caliber revolver. The coroner ruled the death a suicide. Mickey commented, "But not over this," referring to the Nixon campaigns. The case remains unsolved.
10. When Raft was having tax problems, Neddie Herbert asked Mickey to return the favor by giving Raft the necessary short funds; he did. A reporter once asked an elder Raft what had happened to all his millions. His answer: "Part of the loot when for gambling, part for horses, and part for women. The rest I spent foolishly."
11. Dave Chasen, who started at Mocambo, remained friends with Sinatra. When he first opened his restaurant, it served spareribs for thirty-four cents and chili for twenty-five. Director Frank Capra called the hangout Chasen's Southern Barbecue Pit. Chasen's, by then serving its signature Hobo Steak and iced seafood tower, would become a second home to the Rat Pack, the Reagans, and countless executives.
12. Mickey relied on lifelong friend Artie Samish for protective state connections. Samish, a politician-fixer-lobbyist, did not know Mickey from the neighborhood, as many true-crime writers have claimed. Los Angeles-born Samish spent most of his youth in San Francisco, and was approximately fifteen years older than

Mickey. "A meaty individual of some three hundred pounds, Samish has an interesting political credo himself, which he once expressed as, 'To hell with the governor of the state; I am the governor of the legislature'"—Burton Turkus and Sid Feder. Samish once posed with a dummy to illustrate how he controlled the puppet California government. The California State Brewers Institute paid the chubby Samish $30,000 a year, with a slush fund of $150,000 more. He received another $36,000 from Schenley Distillers in New York. He made close to $1,000,000 in only six years. The IRS and Senator Estes Kefauver relied on telephone company records to establish that Samish was a crook. "Next to Hollywood and oranges, Samish is California's biggest crop for export"—Jack Lait and nephew Lee Mortimer. He acted as the inside contact for real estate moguls. When Kefauver investigated him, he told the committee that he threw away all his canceled checks. For Treasury agents, he added, "and the waste-basket is in my safe." "He is a combination of Falstaff, Little Boy Blue, and Machiavelli, crossed with an eel"—Estes Kefauver. Samish, who liked to wear bright-banded straw hats, would do time in prison for tax evasion. His case went to the U.S. Supreme Court, where Chief Justice Earl Warren removed himself from the hearing.

13. The Burbank land was originally part of two large Spanish grants, one in 1798 and the other in 1821. Dr. David Burbank, a dentist, purchased portions of both ranches totaling 4,000 acres. Lockheed moved in, and later produced 19,000 planes during World War II. First National

Pictures purchased a seventy-acre site and later sold it to the four Warner brothers. Columbia Pictures followed, as did Walt Disney.

14. Arthur "Mickey" McBride, who had worked for wire-founder Annenberg, took the reins of the Continental Press Service in 1939. McBride, the first owner of the Cleveland Browns football team, would tell the Kefauver committee in 1951 that he started the business "on a modest bankroll of $20,000 purely out of sentiment and goodwill to provide a job for my brother-in-law, [Tom] Kelly," whom Kefauver made a point of calling "bald and seemingly disingenuous." "I didn't buy anything from Nation Wide, not so much as a toothpick... I started a new business," confirmed McBride. Kefauver illustrated that the investment paid off several hundred fold in a matter of months. The Chicago mob naturally had wanted to cut itself in on the operation.

15. Most critics ignored the historical inaccuracy of the movie, a story line taken from the then twenty-five-year-old Dean Jennings' anecdotal biography of Bugsy.

16. Del Webb would become involved in several casino ventures, including the Sahara Hotel. He helped build many of the city's municipal facilities and retirement communities.

17. Los Angeles flooring contractor John Biren had meetings with Tony Cornero, who had started the Stardust Company. Cornero would only meet at odd hours. Biren and his partner, with carpet samples in hand for the hotel, went to Cornero's residence at one in the morning. Cornero argued with his mother over the samples, finally

yelling to her, "Who the fuck asked you?" Then he turned to Biren and calmly stated, "You will take stock." Biren logically and bravely explained that he couldn't afford to wait for payment, and left unscathed. When assassins shot Cornero outside his Beverly Hills home, the police questioned Mickey, who told them that Tony was an upstanding citizen in the Mexican meat business. When the Stardust officially opened in 1955, the guests of honor were future president LBJ and protégé political secretary Bobby Baker.

Chapter 4

[18]. In 1963 builders demolished the luxurious late nineteenth century Hollenden Hotel to make way for a box-like modern structure.

[19]. Well-built Hill, also known as Ginny, was the daughter of a cocktail-friendly Alabama marble polisher of Slovak descent. She lived a tomboy existence with her grandmother on a Georgia cotton farm, learning to ride horses and swim naked. She quit school at fourteen, and three years later made a showing as a young woman on the Midway at the Chicago World's Fair, in a show called "Elephants and Fleas." Before she met Bugsy, she had been married four times in sixteen years. One of these spouses was Chicago betting commissioner Joe Epstein. He wasn't rich enough for her, although he received a cut from every bookie in town. Epstein, a protégé of Greasy Thumb Guzik, ran the mob's wire service. Through unattractive Mr. Magoo-ish Epstein, Hill met mobsters Frank Nitti, Tony Accardo, the

Fischetti brothers, Joe Adonis, Frank Costello, and Lucky Luciano. Her mating ran the gamut from Mexican rumba dancers to Austrian skiers. Known for her flamboyant tendencies, she often dropped ten grand a night for parties, and she once convinced Bugsy to invest in a poppy-growing business. The FBI coldly referred to Hill as a thrice-married obscene dope addict. Many considered her only a mob courier, her duties no more sophisticated than a bagman's. She sometimes carried sums in the millions. When she talked Sam Goldwyn into a part in *Ball of Fire*, directed by Howard Hawks, she had hit the big time. In the company of stars Gary Cooper, Barbara Stanwyck, Oscar Homolka, Henry Travers, S. Z. Sakall, Dan Duryea, Elisha Cook, Jr., and Dana Andrews at the Grauman's Chinese premier, Hill strolled up with her escort Bugsy Siegel. Bugsy's wife Esther headed back to Brooklyn with the Siegel daughters, and soon agreed to a Reno divorce, netting $32,000 per year. Bugsy and Hill had a rocky relationship. She abused sleeping pills, and often ended up in emergency rooms, followed by oodles of bad publicity. She starved herself to remain thin. "He's [Bugsy] very overbearing. He always wants his own way. I'm used to having my own way, too, and we're apt to have lots of battles"—Virginia Hill. She appeared before the Kefauver hearings on March 15, 1951, and overdosed on sleeping pills in 1966.

[20]. The house belonged to Juan Romero, Rudolph Valentino's manager.

[21]. Mickey's routine included a minimum of one Cadillac in front and one behind his vehicle.

When he went out at night, the caravan would circle his restaurant destination. One vehicle would peel off at a time, and his boys would check out the inside of the restaurant while the rest of the vehicles continued around the block. The circling repeated, with Mickey's car pulling in to the parking lot last. Los Angeles folklore maintains that he would use the same method for returning to the Boyle Heights Cornwall Street Synagogue, where he would say Kaddish for his father. The Cadillac was the chosen vehicle for the mob. The sons of mobsters, who sometimes were able to take the cars on dates, referred to the sleek machines as Dadillacs, and dressed to the nines with pinky rings to impress their hot dates.

22. Costello began in the mid 1920s as a sub-capo in the Manhattan Joe Maseria family. His brethren included Lucky Luciano, Vito Genovese, Albert Anastasia, Joe Adonis, Anthony Anastasia, Carlo Gambino, and Willie Moretti. Those mobsters avoided the public eye, while Arnold Rothstein, Dutch Schultz, Legs Diamond, Owney Madden, and Bill Dwyer made headlines. Costello's mentor was Rothstein. In 1929, playground Atlantic City played host to Costello, Luciano, Lepke (who controlled the garment center), Adonis, Johnny Torrio, Lou Rothkopf, Moe Dalitz, King Solomon, John Lazia, Joe Bernstein, Sam Lazar, and kingpin Al Capone. The Traymore Hotel hosted the cigar-chomping organizers, who took time out to scan the white beaches for girls sporting the new fashion—bathing suits above the knee. During the Kefauver Hearings, Costello refused to be

televised, allowing only his moving hands to be photographed, suggesting what some called a "hand ballet." He would eventually retire, and commute from his Long Island mansion to his New York apartment.

Chapter 5

1. Under the guidance of East Coast interests, the Flamingo showed a $4,000,000 profit at the end of the year, after skimming $15,000,000 (according to the authors Giancana). The Flamingo and later the Desert Inn would easily outdo the El Rancho, and attract national attention to redrawing the landscape of Las Vegas. The city moved along, and ten neon-lit casinos soon spotted the desert, increasing in short order to thirteen. Jake Katleman, Tutor Scherer, Guy McAfee, Farmer Page, Bill Curland, Chuck Addison, and other high-profile gamblers migrated to Vegas from L.A., while New York's Frank Costello, the Chicago Fischettis, the Detroit Liccavolis, Brooklyn's Joe Adonis, and New Jersey's Longie Zwillman watched their investment in the Flamingo soar.
2. Since 1946, Governor Warren had been working on an Organized Crime Commission; he received final approval in 1947. Squeaky-clean Warren continued his commission. He smelled something fishy about Howser's campaign compatriots. Howser had sent John Riggs and Wiley "Buck" Caddel to investigate bookmaking. Riggs doctored his reports and the courts convicted Caddel and retired Los Angeles police officer James M. "Chinese" Mulligan for bribery and conspiracy

to violate gambling laws. Caddel was part of the $2,000,000,000 slot business, with $400,000,000 allocated for protection.
3. The *Nation* was founded in 1865, and declared it would not be the "organ of any party, sect, or body." It remains a left-leaning, liberal periodical.
4. An odd example of Mickey's creative interests involves an author of children's stories who had met him. When he learned that she was traveling to Boston, he arranged for her to meet Rocky Paladino, who escorted her around town. The Damon Runyon character inspired her, and she subsequently wrote a series of children's stories about him and his stable of horses.
5. Hecht had been an acrobat, magician, newspaperman, playwright, author, and screenwriter before meeting Mickey. Some of his many screenplays were *Gunga Din, Wuthering Heights, Scarface, Notorious, Spellbound*, and *The Front Page*; perhaps half of all the great Hollywood movies, according to critic Pauline Kael. He was also famous on the literary scene: he authored books, plays, and an extensive number of short stories.
6. The Irgun, a derivative of the kibbutz-based Haganah, was a Jewish defense organization that began with the imprimatur of the British to help with Arab rebellions in the late thirties. By the forties, British policy toward Jews changed dramatically, and the British forced Jewish refugees to live in Australian internment camps behind barbed wire. One year after the start of WW II, the British government arrested 75,000 Jews, citing them as "enemy aliens." Survivors

of the HMT *Dunera*, a ship that brought about 2,000 Jews to Australia, still meet each year near the dock in Sydney where the ship had arrived. Two years after *Dunera*, the British reversed their position and publicly admitted that they had made a "deplorable mistake." The Haganah developed its attack corps, the Palmach, and the main revisionist group, the Irgun Zvai Leumi; the two operated under similar charters. The major distinction was the Irgun's policy of openly condoning terrorist attacks against the British, including killing officials and hostages. "…initially the Israelis were poorly armed, inadequately trained, and disorganized, but the officers of their liberation army, drawn almost entirely from the kibbutzim, in the end prevailed"—Norman Cantor. The Irgun made international headlines after blowing up the British military headquarters at the King David Hotel in Jerusalem. The Irgun fighters had entered the basement of the hotel disguised as employees and the explosives were hidden in milk cans. A warning phone call informed the British: either get out or be blown up. Sir John Shaw answered, "I am here to give orders to the Jews, not to receive orders from them." He eventually left with a few of his top officers. The Irgun destroyed the British headquarters and archives.

7. Preminger more likely sought expert advice from Mickey during the preproduction period of one of his earlier film noir movies like *Where The Sidewalk Ends*, about a cop killing a murder suspect, or *Whirlpool*, about a shoplifter married to a psychiatrist, perhaps even *Angel Face*, about a woman who kills her lover.

Chapter 6

1. Hecht was comfortable with his Jewish origins but did not become an activist until 1939. He had "turned into a Jew...some 45 years after his bris."—Sidney Zion.
2. "The more guns, the better chance for game, so overseas solicitors are frequently brought in for the attack."—Gerald Krefetz.
3. "The techniques range from appealing to the most profound Jewish instinct of charity by using the most flagrant and cynical panhandling techniques of the schnorer. It pulls out all the stops, from pathos to bathos, and cashes in on every emotion."—Gerald Krefetz. "There are rules to this game as in any other. When out for big trophies, a safari is the preferred hunting method. It is an accepted principle that one man should never go alone to solicit a major gift. It is too easy to say no to one man, especially if he is a friend or neighbor. When two or more go, it is no longer one Jew asking another for a gift—it is the entire community, it is the Jewish people."—Paul Zuckerman.
4. The *Altalena* carried 900 people, including Menachem Begin, 5,000 rifles, 450 machine guns, and enough ammunition to fuel a significant battle, according to author Rockaway. While other sources report different numbers, the fact remains that the ship was loaded for war, heavily assisted by the Jewish mob. The Irgun was intent on docking the vessel, despite warnings from the Israeli government and the United Nations. *Time* magazine reported on the

June 25, 1948, altercation: "Bitterest Blow. On the beach at Kfar Vitkin, 20 miles north of Tel Aviv, waited slight, sharp-eyed Menachim Beigin [Menachem Begin] and a force of his bully boys, to help unload." The Haganah, now Israel's official army, was waiting with orders to stop them. The result was a short, sharp civil war of Jew against Jew, which Prime Minister David Ben-Gurion described as "the bitterest blow." Some historians wrote that the argument had more to do with how to distribute the materials. Ben-Gurion insisted that the Irgun be part of the one nation-one army theory, with no special privileges, everything divided equally. He was afraid that a civil war would erupt, but started one anyway. The terrorists partially unloaded the cargo at Kfar Vitkin, and lost six, twenty wounded, while the Haganah suffered fewer losses. Begin boarded the ship, and ordered it southward. At midnight, the *Altalena* rammed the beach at Tel Aviv. At noon, an assault boat with a few armed Irgunists headed for the beach and set up a mini-beachhead amidst small-arms fire. On orders from Prime Minister Ben-Gurion, the army shelled the ship and it caught fire. Correspondents and U.N. observers had been watching from the balcony of the Kaete Dan Hotel. By morning, the soldiers had destroyed the ship, and forty died.

5. Russian journalist Jabotinsky was the father of the Revisionist (New) Zionist Movement and the associated Betar youth camps. He died of a heart attack during a trip to a Betar summer camp in upstate New York in 1940. He had fought for the formation of a Jewish state on both sides of the

Jordan River and was against any partition plans for the new nation. He was one of the greatest proponents of the Hebrew language. Denied reentry into Palestine by the British in 1929, his remains were ultimately returned to Jerusalem in 1965.

6. The soldiers fought alongside the British as the Zion Mule Corps at the battle of Gallipoli and in North Africa directly against the Nazis.

7. Actor Walter Matthau told this story to movie producer Eliot Kastner at the Beverly Hills Tennis Club. "A lot of things were being stolen at a shtetl in Israel. There was one suspect, but the residents decided the best thing to do was have the rabbi settle the dilemma. The rabbi confronted the thief and made a suggestion, 'If you want a new life I can arrange for you to move over the hill to the shtetl on the east side, and you can start a new life there. I've talked with their rabbi, and it can be arranged.' The young man was very grateful and agreed to move. About one year later, the rabbi received a message from the east side rabbi, 'We are continually losing our silver and gold. Please take him back.' The young man returned to the original shtetl, and stood before his old rabbi, head bowed, ashamed. The rabbi spoke in a deep, solemn voice, 'How can you have done this after the opportunity I have provided for you?' The man thought for a moment and answered as if he had made a brilliant discovery, 'I guess I'm just a thief, rabbi.'"

8. The structure of many charities lends itself to the kind of creative accounting commonplace in Mickey's business. Charities have been notorious

for expenses associated with operations. It is conceivable for someone like Mickey to skim some of the proceeds, but unlikely in this case since it was a national mob venture. In addition, the Jewish fundraising machine was as powerful and as well organized as Mickey's mob. They would never have stood by and watched the money disappear. In addition, Mickey's exaggerated payroll was now a whopping $500,000 a day, with his take estimated as high as $250,000 after expenses. A ton of cash floated around the country, and although skimming wasn't the worst crime, particularly amongst criminals, Mickey and the Jewish mob did not need to defraud the Zionist organizations.

9. Irish Vernon Ferguson was tall with white hair, and was an imposing presence in the courtroom. He would head up the Los Angeles County grand jury for three decades.

Chapter 7

10. Sinatra continually relied on the mob. His lifelong gangster friendships intertwined his social life with Hollywood mob life. He didn't take his legendary breakups well. When he split with Lauren Bacall (Betty Perske), he chose the telephone to deliver the bad news. He had difficulty facing former girlfriends, and developed a solid "Hit the road, Jack!" attitude, isolating himself from most. If any of the women persisted in pursuing him, he would ask attorney Mickey Rudin to step in and Rudin hammered home the stay-away message with cold legal letters. Sinatra was not fond of "spoiled

Jew brats," and dated none of the locals. When Bacall fell out of favor, she became "the Jew bitch." He wasn't shy about describing her lack of talent in the fellatio arena: "All she does is whistle." Aside from Bacall, his only other Jewish love was Jill St. John (Jill Oppenheim), who after indoctrination with George Raft proved a perfect mob match for Sinatra, who loved gangster dialogue. Sinatra didn't date black women, although he was no stranger to black call girls, a steady stream of which was readily available. He would quip, "Trade you two vanillas for one chocolate." One night he tried to entice Judith Exner into a ménage a trois with a naked black guest who appeared unexpectedly and began performing fellatio on him in front of her.

11. D'Amato never graduated from elementary school, and started out with a small gambling operation. His 500 Club was renowned for its headliners and mobsters, and he for his gambling and pimping skills. He was no stranger to Giancana and Lucky Luciano, maintained a lifelong friendship with Sinatra (helped him when his career was flailing), and promoted Jack Kennedy to win the primary in West Virginia.

12. Throughout his life, Sinatra referred to Dean as "the wop." Jerry Lewis was always "the Jew," Laurence Harvey was "Ladyboy," Cary Grant was "Sheenie," and Johnny Mathis was "the African Queen." Sinatra's private plane was *El Dago*. Comedian Jan Murray, who occasionally appeared first at Sinatra's concerts, was only greeted by "Hey, Clyde." George Jacobs, Sinatra's African-American assistant, tolerated "spook."

Between the mafia-speak and "ring-a-ding-dings," only insiders knew the entire code. When Sinatra felt it was appropriate, he could turn on the charm and the altar boy sensibilities.

13. Egoless Dean Martin, always friendly with Mickey, was born in mob-tolerant Steubenville, Ohio (population 20,000), where casinos, speakeasies, and brothels operated freely. He had dealt cards and boxed (Kid Crochet), but preferred his singing waiter jobs at mob-run clubs. "I had a great time growing up in Steubenville. There was everything a boy could want. Women. Music. Nightclubs. Liquor. And to think I had all that when I was only thirteen"—Dean Martin. "…he was a good guy, very easy to get along with…he was rough, uncouth, not educated—I don't think he ever read a book"—Herman Zlotchover (Hover). Hover also took credit for Martin and Lewis' rise in popularity, but admitted that Martin solidified his career through his mob relationships. "The mobsters tolerated Jerry, but they loved Dean; they courted him, seeking his company in saloons and casinos and on golf courses… Dean knew that the world for such men was a one-way arrangement; he was smart enough to never be disrespectful or insubordinate—asked to make an appearance, he usually complied—but he kept his distance and tried to maintain strictly professional relationships with any gangsters who wanted to get closer"—Shawn Levy. Lucky Luciano once lobbied Sinatra to induce Dean to play Luciano in a movie about his life. It never came to fruition; Dean begged off, he had his limits.

During his declining years, La Famiglia restaurant owner Joe Patti would take Dean's dentures and hide them behind the bar. He preferred to drink without them. Dean entertained locals with endless stories, mostly about his golf exploits.

14. Jerry Lewis makes no mention of Mickey in his recent memoir. He did include New York boss Frank Costello, the Fischetti brothers, Gus Greenbaum, Willie Moretti, and Bugsy. He had admitted previously that Mickey might have arranged the Martin and Lewis debut, but denied Mickey's political assistance with the unions.

15. In return for favors and money, Mickey obliged the unions' suggestions, and was influential in controlling people who worked in and out of the entertainment business. The FBI watched and reported on Mickey's role in the show business unions, "They [Mickey's boys] were instructed to create as much disturbance as possible in order to discredit the strike. They were told to roust and slug persons in the picket lines and if apprehended they were to disclaim membership in any group...use dynamite and if necessary to kill anyone who interfered..."

16. Brenda Allen was one of the most successful madams in town; some referred to her as a prostitute, since she ran a stable with hundreds of girls. Her clients included movie stars and gangsters. Popular Allen had her name, picture, and telephone number printed in the Official Players Directory published by the Academy of Motion Picture Arts and Sciences. She had a stable of 114 girls, and it was not unusual for each girl to gross $1200 per day. Allen worked

on a 50% split. She subscribed to doctors' and lawyers' telephone answering services, and made sure every cab driver, bartender, and bellhop had her direct line. Her Hollywood love-for-sale nests, as the newspapers called them, were an integral part of the social scene.

[17]. When things died down, *Newsweek* followed a social story about Mickey and his girlie friends. The sultry blondes, Vicki Evans and Lila Leeds, decked out in elegant outfits, posed for photographers. Lila draped a fancy fur stole, complete with the little mink's head, over her wide-lapelled jacket. The D.A. later charged her with membership in a call-girl setup. She, of course, denied the charges.

[18]. Many illegal abortion clinics existed throughout the United States until 1973, the year the Supreme Court legalized it. The costly illegal procedures often took place in unsanitary conditions with staffs of unqualified midwives and scam artists.

[19]. Other authors prefer a less popular version: later in the afternoon on a sunny California day, Mickey and henchman Frankie Niccoli waltzed into a restaurant across from Paramount Pictures, and then beat Utley.

Chapter 8

[1]. Mickey made a foray into the oil business in Wichita Falls, Texas, but trouble with the Texas Rangers put a damper on his pursuits in the area.

[2]. Meltzer had come out west after his "New Joisey" pal Charlie "The Jew" Janowsky, a successful gambler, was ice-picked to death and left to

drain. Since Meltzer knew Neddie, it was a natural to work for Mickey. Meltzer ran a jewelry store near Mickey's haberdashery.
3. So much graft filtered through the police department, that one officer had enough money to build a $100,000-dollar hotel.
4. Harry Grossman, of the Ruditsky Detective Agency, introduced Vaus to Mickey. Vaus worked for the police and Mickey at the same time—an undoubtedly favorable situation for Mickey. To make the initial switch, Mickey gave Vaus $300 in cash, a woman's diamond ring, chrome auto accessories, and suits and ties. Vaus exposed everything that he had done for the police to Mickey, including the location of his residential bugs.
5. Total bail estimates hit a high of $300,000 for Mickey and his gang. He posted $75,000 bonds for Frankie Niccoli and Davey Ogul. He had to collateralize his Brentwood home and cars to cover the bail. An FBI report stated that Mickey never reported income of more than $15,000 a year, causing agents to wonder how he came up with the bail money.
6. "Vice men have a bad public reputation. The public thinks we are just a bunch of bulls sneaking around to break up somebody's friendly Friday night poker game"—Captain Charles Stanley.
7. Garner was an established movie actress who began work as a child contemporary of Roddy McDowall. Her most famous theatrical work was her yearlong tour in *Bus Stop*, where she met and married leading man Albert Salmi. Her portrayal of Francis Nolan in Kazan's adaptation of the

Betty Smith novel *A Tree Grows In Brooklyn* earned Garner a special juvenile Oscar.

8. Glaser had worked for the famous Music Corporation of America, a forerunner of MCA. MCA's impressive client list included Louis Armstrong and Billie Holiday.

9. Jim Richardson had originally asked Mickey to feed him occasional tips regarding anything newsworthy. The cordial relationship that developed instead helped sell millions of newspapers over an eighteen-year period.

Chapter 9

1. *Laugh In* television producer George Schlatter was the "bagman" who transferred the Ciro's protection money to Mickey. His job was to take a bag, "a small, heavy, knotted white sack," from the nightclub's show producer, author Weller's Uncle Herman Hover, and walk it into the kitchen. One of Mickey's men would wait there with several of the haberdashery boxes from Mickey's store. Schlatter claims, "As far as I was concerned, I was legitimately buying boxes!" He did say that the boxes appeared devoid of garments.

2. Biscailuz would use Mickey as a focal point for reelection—Vote for me and I'll get rid of Cohen. Every night the sheriff's boys would frisk Mickey and anyone within a football field of the haberdashery or Continental Café on Santa Monica Boulevard. Since this part of the Strip and West Hollywood was still unincorporated, it fell under the larger jurisdiction of Sheriff

Biscailuz, who was forever trying as hard as Mickey to maintain a favorable public image.
3. Ruditsky had opened a detective agency in Hollywood, and fancied himself an expert on the mob; Chief of Police Anderson of Beverly Hills questioned him after Bugsy's murder. Clients like Bugsy, Mickey, and Al Smiley had used him as a glorified bill collector. Ruditsky's exploits with partner Johnny Broderick became the hard-as-nails stuff of crime writers. Ruditsky died on October 18, 1962. Although a detective, his extensive obit outlined his almost fictional association with crime, culminating with consulting work on television and movies.
4. Stompanato had run gift, pet, furniture stores, and even sold cars.
5. Ballistic experts corroborated that the guns used in the Sherry's shooting were loaded with "heavy slugs," also called a .30-06 bullet, legal in some states for deer hunting, and consistent with Neddie and Mickey's injuries.
6. The whole setup smelled amateurish: a vacant lot was the worst choice to stage operations. Residents would later report that the escape route wasn't organized either. As the shooters raced down Hammond Street after pulling out of a dead-end, getaway cars nearly collided with the lookout car. Where were the shooters aiming? A better name for the L.A. mob, instead of "The Mickey Mouse Mafia," could be "The Gang That Couldn't Shoot Straight," a title once used by gonzo journalist Jimmy Breslin to describe the Crazy Joe Gallo wiseguys.

7. Another FBI memorandum half-heartedly tried to discredit Mickey and the attention directed toward him after the Sherry's shooting: "Cohen is commonly reputed to be a braggart who, at least until the recent past, was anxious to be esteemed as a notorious "tough" and it appears probable that the discrepancies between his admitted arrests and those reflected in his identification record arose from a feeble attempt on his part to deceive the…agents as to his actual arrest record."
8. Mayor Bowron had summoned Worton, a retired major general in the Marine Corps, from San Diego when Chief Horrall suddenly took ill in the aftermath of the heated Brenda Allen events. Horrall resigned, content to collect his $572 monthly pension. Police Chief Reed also resigned after the final six-week grand jury inquiry into the corruption of the LAPD.
9. Recent versions of the Sherry's shooting do not always jibe with the newspapers or practical knowledge of mob operations. What appeared confusing in author Sheila Weller's delicious story about her family and Ciro's is the interpretation of "protection money." When referring to Mickey's local rackets she writes, "…he was extorting some kind of protection money from my uncle. (The protection money, however, didn't keep Cohen from getting shot in the shoulder outside Ciro's in 1949 by a rival gangster, who killed one of Cohen's lieutenants and wounded U.S. attorney general's agent, who was guarding Cohen after he'd 'flipped' to the feds' side in a mob prosecution.)" Her Uncle Herman didn't pay Mickey protection money so

that *he* would protect Mickey. Most sources do not refer to Ciro's, today the Comedy Store, as the shooting location.

Chapter 10

1. Underwood would hold the title of Hearst City Editor. Despite her popularity, the all-male Greater L.A. Press Club denied her membership.
2. J. Edgar Hoover was approximately in the middle of a forty-eight-year run as head of the FBI. His helpful prevailing attitude toward Mickey and the mob permeated the Bureau. He always maintained that organized crime was a local problem; he called the mob and Mafia "baloney" (in behind-closed-doors parlance, bullshit) and insisted that local crime was a function of lax police departments. He was a statistics nut, who loved to brag about his success with bank robberies, car thefts, kidnappings, and white-collar cases. The system under Hoover "...could pick and chose which cases you wanted to prosecute."—Curt Gentry. Hoover never picked Mickey, despite years of FBI underling work to nail him. When challenged, the FBI cited a lack of evidence.
3. J. Howard McGrath succeeded outgoing Attorney General Tom C. Clark. Both worked under President Harry S. Truman, and had to respect the president and Hoover's stand on Mickey.

Chapter 11

1. Mickey took full advantage of his continued celebrity. He kept his social lists and like the

movie moguls sent out over 300 gift baskets for the holidays, mostly to poor families. His old card-playing pal Charlie Shuster, from the Jim Dandy supermarkets, saw to the gift-giving.

[2]. The 452 miles remained a patchwork, without any prior planning. When a piece of land became available, the city annexed it, increasing the sprawling and therefore uncontrollable urban expanse. Numerous tiny independent municipalities existed like Beverly Hills, little islands of land that fell under Los Angeles county jurisdiction, many easily manipulated by Mickey.

[3]. Addicted gambler Mike Todd, part owner of the track at Del Mar, married Elizabeth Taylor, and was tragically killed in a plane crash one year later.

[4]. Superior Court Judge Thomas Ambrose had ruled that Mickey's attorneys did not prove that Niccoli was dead. Dee David had found Niccoli's car at the municipal airport back in September. Ogul's car turned up at UCLA, where a student witnessed Ogul leave in another vehicle. The judge told Mickey that he would have ninety days to come up with information that is more pertinent. He also issued a warrant for Niccoli's arrest as a bond-jumper. Mickey could not help the court obtain any additional information, and therefore lost the money, guaranteed by the Massachusetts Bonding Company.

[5]. Detective Wellpott eventually retired because his wife received threatening phone calls for two years. Intelligence Squad Sergeant Jerry Wooters blamed Mickey for his ulcer.

6. The house was located at 513 Moreno, still a very chic address today, a kissing cousin of Beverly Hills and Bel-Air. The interior colors were lemon, mauve, and shocking blue. Ex-con Jim Vaus (J. Arthur Vaus), "King of the Wiretappers," and a future evangelist, installed a radar system to warn of unwelcome guests, remote control garage door openers, and floodlights, for $3,000. The warning device signaled a buzzer located over the bar. The house also periodically had phone taps and bugs installed by either the Los Angeles police or the FBI, likely the first time by Vaus during initial repairs. Hidden microphones lined the walls of every room, including the swanky bathrooms.
7. Mickey often left town with $30,000 cash in tow. He traveled lavishly, and spent fifteen grand per trip, but in the process would pick up gambling markers totaling over $20,000. He could be nine grand short one moment and suddenly collect twenty-four the same day.
8. Mickey had called Moe Sedway at the Flamingo to patch up their differences, and call off the estrangement that had begun when they had fought years back. He knew that he couldn't isolate himself from Sedway, whom Lansky admired. He had asked Moe Sedway to help locate the gambler who owed the money. The FBI mentioned that Sedway caught the flu during this period and had spent a few days in the hospital—typical of the inconsequential details interspersed inside thousands of reports.
9. A Packard auto dealer founded KFI, one of the first television stations. It survives as a

radio station, while its original Channel 9 slot has new call letters.

10. Dean Jagger, a former Ohio farm boy and schoolteacher, was famous for his roles in *Twelve O'Clock High* (which earned him an Oscar for his performance opposite Gregory Peck) and *Rawhide*.

11. "Attempting determine relationship between Cohen and officers in Wilshire Div..." was one of the FBI's many communications. The FBI ultimately did figure out that the Wilshire Division of the L.A.P.D. had employed Mickey and his torpedoes to intimidate Pearson. They concluded that the police had held a grudge against Pearson, and Mickey's role was to settle the score. Any further federal attempts to unravel Mickey's police relationships proved unsuccessful.

Made in the USA
Coppell, TX
11 November 2022

86221518R10164